OPTIMUM DRIVE

"This is NOT just a book about driving! It literally is the Zen of teaching, internal assessment, and personal growth. Paul's years of coaching, (including me) have paid off in a must read for anyone pursuing limits beyond their comfort zone. Don't buy this book to drive better – buy it to be a BETTER PERSON and to find what makes you tick...No kidding! Oh yea, and you can drive faster!"

- Bob Miller, 2001 World Challenge Rookie of the Year and Volvo NA Race Team Owner

"As an aspiring racer and lifetime student of performance driving, I've thoroughly enjoyed and benefited from Optimum Drive. Paul's writing is full of insights -- both into the psychology of competitive driving – and drive itself - accompanied with some very powerful and useable techniques. The way he brings to life the role of tires and the concept of 'Zerosteer' improved my lap times. From his decades of experience, this book delivers on its promise to make you smarter, better and faster."

— Chris Cappy, President, Pilot Consulting Corporation

"Optimum Drive is a racers guide for anyone trying to get to the top tiers of professional motor racing. As a professional driving coach Paul has seen a wide range of driver issues and understands the complexity of modern motorsports and its technological components. Paul explains the areas a driver must focus his efforts on to master his craft."

- D. Bruce Reichel, Racer and Career Driving Trainer, Driving SME

"I have been involved in high performance driving, including club racing, at all amateur levels for twenty-five years. No professional I have been exposed to in numerous driving and racing schools over the years has articulated, demonstrated and taught high-performance driving and race-craft knowledge and skills better than Paul Gerrard."

-Gary Church, President & CEO of Aviation Management Associates, Inc.

"Have you tried driving an automobile at the limit of performance on a track... naked?

Paul Gerrard's comprehensive principles overlay a method of drilling down to the truth of your skill set. You get in the car, take your fire suit off, and get blasted by a pressure washer. Sure this sounds painful, but you're washing in the honesty of driver skills assessment.

In doing so you grow—performing at a higher level— going beyond the plateau that you never realized you were stuck on.

Reading Paul's book is an insightful and welcomed experience. Optimum Drive stands apart from the crowd of how-to-drive-a-race-car publications."

-Rob Schermerhorn, Delta Vee Motorsports LLC

Optimum Drive

THE ROADMAP TO DRIVING GREATNESS

Paul F. Gerrard

PROFESSIONAL DRIVER

For permission requests, please contact the publisher at:
Mango Publishing Group
2850 Douglas Road, 3rd Floor
Coral Gables, FL 33134 USA
info@mango.bz

For special orders, quantity sales, course adoptions and corporate sales,
please email the publisher at sales@mango.bz. For trade and wholesale
sales, please contact Ingram Publisher Services at customer.service@
ingramcontent.com or +1.800.509.4887.

Optimum Drive: The Roadmap to Driving Greatness

Library of Congress Cataloging-in-Publication has been applied for.
ISBN: (paperback) 978-1-63353-517-6, (ebook) 978-1-63353-518-3
BISAC category code SPO041000 SPORTS & RECREATION /
Sports Psychology

Printed in the United States of America

"I have no Idols, I respect work, dedication and competence."

- Ayrton Senna

Table of Contents

Preface

Preface

Timing is Everything/The Devil is in the Detail

PART THREE
Anticipation vs. Reaction
Advanced Skills
Video Power
Appendix

AUTHOR

Paul and I met up many years ago at the Jim Russell Racing Driver's School where we both had an association. I still remember vividly sitting listening to him in the classroom where he perfectly described the intricate balancing act the car and driver do at the first moment the brake pedal is pressed, through to the apex, applying power and the corner exit. It was obvious that he had a way of bringing the interaction of man and machine into words and sensations that we can then translate into lap time.

This book pulls on all of those world experiences, on and off track, taking you from the very basics of driving to the qualities and skills you need at the top level. Even if you have won World Championships, all of us can still learn, and the day you stop, is the day you finish second. I promise you'll learn something so read on . . .

Allan McNish, Formula One Driver, Three Times Le Mans Winner, WEC/ALMS Champion, Television commentator and analyst

Foreword

Most people may find the concept of a book about driving, NOT published by the DMV, to be peculiar at best. Living in a "driving culture" where we almost universally have contact with a car or even a steering wheel on a daily basis the thought of reading more than we absolutely have to in order to take advantage of this beautiful freedom might seem asinine. However, while 'Optimum Drive' is more about human potential than human transportation, more about racing than actual driving, I still believe that if for some reason we all had to dribble a basketball to work, the NBA players would be the best commuters out there and we would all be practicing our dribbling skills. So, while this book may not be about daily driving it is rooted in a subject matter that a vast majority of us can relate to on some level even if, sadly, we don't all dream of racing cars.

Fortunately, for those of us who are driving fanatics, 'Optimum Drive' is a tactile guide to improving every aspect of your passion--with a twist: Within these pages driving seems almost like a vehicle to teach ridiculously poignant lessons on living a fuller, more capable life; It's a clear map to accessing and concurring facets of our human condition that typically restrain us behind the wheel and in life. Consequently, after reading this book you may be a much faster, smarter driver but you might also be able to grasp the bosonic string theory and its 26 dimensions of space with a bit more verve.

As a racer and a biology major I find Paul's physiological and psychosomatic perspective of the "driver" strangely refreshing. When driving at the limit it's easy to feel that virtually all of the instincts we have capitalized on to become the most successful specie in our planet's history do exactly nothing for us on a racetrack. Paul leads us through a clear path of logical progression identifying and celebrating parts of this innate wiring not just for their shortcomings in a car but for how they can be utilized to find our true potential. He pulls the veil off of what is sometimes called driving talent, breaking down the ability to learn driving skills into their components while offering a chronology to the lessons that results in an enhanced learning ability. I have always considered the rate that a driver can learn to be a measure of their talent but Paul's concept is viable and awesome!

I've known Paul for nearly 20 years and have always been amazed by his combined acute observation skills and a bizarrely effective ability to communicate. When you mix in a pinch of intellectual juggernaut and a dash of self-effacing humor you have the makings of a great writer that in this book hits the proverbial nail on the head more times than an ironworker.

There are so many tools supplied in 'Optimum Drive' but their virtue is in their accessibility. I have no doubt that after reading this book you'll be surprisingly inspired, as I was, and as soon at the last page closes you'll be off to the kart track for some training!

Tanner Foust, Three Times Global Rallycross Champion, Nine Times X Games Medalist, Two Times Winner of the Formula Drift Championship and Television Automotive Personality/Host

The Vanishing Art
of Greatness

Holistic (/hō'listik/) is one of those new age words that is usually used to describe a form of all-encompassing health care; its meaning, however, goes well beyond medicine and really applies anywhere. It defines how things operate in complex systems and that you cannot describe or understand the individual part unless you understand the system as a whole. It holds our feet to the fire and tells us that greatness is all or nothing, it must at times be earned step by agonizing step. With our constantly distracted lives today, we operate under the illusion that we have evolved into amazing multitaskers; we have actually lost sight of what our potential truly is. To compensate, we as a society continuously lower the bar of what constitutes excellence. We rely on "google" masking for intelligence; we operate as cogs in a giant machine but don't fully understand what the machine actually does or why it exists. We are slowly relinquishing our true potential as we lose that holistic vision.

With the bar lowered, life is indeed easy; we can feel that we are accomplished in more things than prior generations, but it all is as shallow as it is hollow and ultimately unfulfilling. We are wired for so much more, we are wired for potential, for real old-school greatness.

Greatness has many shapes and forms; it is elusive and rare, yet it exists everywhere if you know how and where to look. It is achieved in all walks of life when an individual does something at such a level that it becomes transcendent and becomes art. Greatness is born out of curiosity about our own potential as human beings, and the unusual, some would say obsessive, drive and focus to see it through. 'Good' is easy; 'great' delves so far into the realm of diminishing returns that most almost sensibly fall short. What happens when curiosity fuels obsession, which then ignites into intense unwavering focus? A mentality that takes us beyond the merely good at the expense of nearly every other aspect of our overly complicated lives is a trade that few will gladly make to reach a level that is purely an act of selfishness or of ego, for it is only done for ourselves, because we wonder just how great we could possibly be. Even though that type of motivation pushes someone to the very edge, the result can be beautifully pure and, yes, great, the ultimate reward of someone who possesses **Optimum Drive**.

Why the World Needs Another Driving Book.

Auto Racing, and of course racecar driving, are two of the best examples of an environment that regularly breeds and encourages greatness on all levels. It is a pure objective sport where the winners and losers are bluntly defined every weekend of the season. Due to the harsh reality of Motorsports, much has been written over many decades detailing the various qualities of success; however, while the sport's results are objective, the driving is not. This creates the issue of trying to describe something subjective in an objective way, like trying to describe feelings with math. Because of this, driving books are typically about the mechanics of driving and provide reams of solid physics and math to back up their approach. The correct way to actually drive a vehicle at its limit has been in print for many decades now. Concepts like the friction circle, slip angle, and load transfer have been explained countless times. That begs the question of why isn't everyone who reads one of these books a great driver? Just read the book(s), memorize the finer points, and instant great driver... if only it were so simple.

So why this book, what's different? This book of course uses the physics and geometry (even if it is refreshingly free of math equations!), but it acknowledges that the "secret" to greatness is not about a series of impressive equations, it's really about you and a machine becoming one. We will endeavor to put all of the principles together in this one place so you can move forward with the process embodied here. In researching this book, I have come to the counterproductive conclusion that everything you need to know about driving has been written; the problem is that it is fragmented, and the pieces are scattered amongst many books written by drivers, engineers, physiologists, and psychologists. Piecing all of that together is not easy; they all speak with different voices and come from different backgrounds, and therefore often have seemingly conflicting points of view and perspectives. When you are trying to piece something together from different sources you are required to fill in the gaps and connect everything. It is hard enough assembling a puzzle of many pieces from the same source, let alone from several. Due to these hurdles, gaps invariably exist, and so even though it all is out there, the solution of how to not only define but also possibly achieve greatness remains elusive. With this single-source holistic approach, you will comprehensively understand what steps to take. This is not just a personal journey towards great driving, but also a secret handshake of sorts that gets you into the incredibly elite club of driving greats that has never been talked about in this way in any book. As a matter of fact, strangely enough I don't know of anyone worldwide that has attempted to really define what specifically a great driver is doing differently than a good driver. Sure, they set the car up better (usually with the help of a more capable team), but what are they actually doing at the limit while driving that's different? We will hit this from a lot of directions as this story unfolds and break it down to its most basic level, but the point is: If the car slides one end or the other, that is not the limit of speed for the car in that corner. Great drivers have a bag of tricks that actually allow them to take that same car and consistently squeeze out more grip. It's taking driving to the level of art. That's what greatness really is. It all starts simply with you and your willingness, your gritty determination to put in the incredible amount of work that takes you there. So then how do we get started?

A complete driver who has all the traits listed above, as well as a true athlete's level of fitness, and is driving a car that is well set up for the conditions in that moment can actually appear to be driving at a nearly superhuman level. The superficial take-away from that is they are just somehow "gifted" to that level. When you dig deeper, though, you find that every single one of them put in the work to get there. The bad news then? It doesn't happen overnight. The good news? Greatness is possible for anyone. I truly believe that, and that is the real reason I felt obsessively compelled and, yes, driven to write this book.

To lay down a marker at a true starting point, you really need to figure out who you are before we dive into the finer points of vehicle dynamics. We need to spend time talking about what it is to be a human being trying to do something that is extraordinarily challenging. This "touchy-feely" stuff is not a popular topic and is therefore typically ignored, which is where I think most schools and training go wrong. You see, for this book to be truly effective, it can't just be about the techniques of driving. That would be fine if I were writing software code and knew that input to output would be pure, but filtered through even the most well-meaning human on the planet, information is subjected to dazzling range of interpretation.

You also need to know why. It's great to be given the perfect techniques of supernatural driving, but to truly get buy-in from you, I feel you really need to know why it is the way it is. This way, with enough focused practice, you can actually feel for yourselves what is right. This enables self-sufficiency, the ability for you to simply feel what fast is. To distill it all down, great driving is about your ability to manage your tires. This seemingly simple goal, to be better than the other guys managing tires, is actually a very complex puzzle, because there is a whole car between you and those tires, and it is all done in a very dangerous and uncomfortable environment surrounded by people trying to beat you. I want to help you deconstruct every aspect of driving chapter by chapter and then reconstruct it into greatness...your greatness.

In addition to driving myself, I have been teaching aspiring to ultra-successful racing drivers for over 20 years. Along the way, I have observed the human animal: how we listen, think, interpret, visualize – and, yes, learn – in a dangerous and therefore stressful environment. I can confidently say that everyone I've had the pleasure of teaching absolutely had the best intentions - they all wanted to learn and discover their capabilities. That is where the similarities end. Beyond the desire to succeed, I've observed that people diverge to a staggering degree.

It is awesome from one perspective, but daunting from mine, because I must write this taking all that into consideration. One point to make is that my tone here has to be quite frank, almost blunt. I can't give wiggle room when it comes to laying this out; we naturally gravitate towards the looseness of wiggle room as an excuse not to take something on board or to heart 100% accurately. We will never be great with wiggle room given (just to be kind). So, don't feel like I'm accusing you and thinking you're a lousy example of a human being; know that I am just as guilty of this as any of you, and so I often rightly use myself here as the bad example ... We are in this together, you and I. I am absolutely as likely as the next person to fall into all of the traps that can affect the outcome. I deal with the same fears and ego-driven mistakes as any person. A great deal of what I have learned to deal with and what has led me to writing this book is observation of students to the point of seeing clear patterns emerge, all the while reflecting on those results with introspection to come up with some clarity on what's really happening. Then I modify my teaching and measure the new results, continually refining the process. I have now reached the point (after over 20 years) where the "system" of driving I propose here is complete, with only refinements being added now.

That's great and all, but the problem here is that this is in the form of a book, so I'm left in the dark with no feedback from you whatsoever; and, well... that's a huge challenge for both of us.

This is something that is far too relevant to, and influential on your success or failure to ignore, especially since, while I write this with the best intentions, I am not sitting next to you in the car. That puts a much more significant burden on you and your self-analysis; you interpret every word here as a well-intentioned person, but with a unique perspective. Again, and one final time, this is not a criticism of my students, of you, or of myself. It is just reality. You must admit this to yourself... Your absolute blunt objectivity is critical.

So, what is the trap we all tend to fall into? You will naturally be attracted to what you feel is important and place less emphasis on what you deem to be not as important. That seemingly innocent priority list will have a profound effect on your success. You need to weigh everything here equally. Since we have a strong ego-driven tendency to put more weight on what we can relate to, what we already feel we are comfortable with, and what we feel we are already good at, we naturally filter out our weaknesses! We want to focus specifically on our weaknesses and put more (certainly not less) emphasis on them. Don't fall into that ego-driven trap.

That's why you and I need to be very careful here. We need to be methodical and spend time talking about things in a specific order to build a solid foundation, while making sure we haven't enshrined some fundamental untruth that later will have a profound negative effect on your abilities, quite possibly forever.

I understand if you are now thinking "come on, enough with the psychobabble, let's just get to the driving part;" as stated, there are plenty of driving books that do just that. I am not that type of driver or coach. I don't want to start with any assumption about (unique) you. I have to lay out my method and how I analyze every student I come into contact with in a way that you can objectively self-analyze and use to end up at the driving portion in the right frame of mind, with the back story and therefore self-confidence to know, really know, that you have all the tools necessary for success. Since we are human, the techniques of how to drive the car are only a small part of success; if that were not the case, everyone would be great, right? Many people assume that maybe it's our physical differences that separate us, things like our reflexes and eyesight, but I can tell you through experience that they are not that important. The mental side of it is an overwhelming percentage of being able to do this well. It's not like weight lifting, where you need years to develop muscle mass, or football or basketball, where there are ideal body types. Really anyone can become fit enough to drive one to two hours in a decent racecar – remember that people with real disabilities have become competitive, capable drivers. Now, I'm not trying to discount the advantages of fitness (there's a whole chapter on it later). I'm just trying to point out that the mental side needs continuous work, much more than any other piece of the puzzle, if greatness is ever going to be achieved.

Now you might be thinking that the pro drivers you follow don't appear to work very hard at being fast. That is just what they want you to think; that's the image they want to cultivate. The whole idea, partly born out of necessity, is to project a complete lack of needing practice or preparation; it's a bit of an ego thing, but it's more of an image-builder and a competitor psych-out tool. There is nothing cooler than showing utter nonchalance, that "whatever" mentality, and projecting that far and wide to the fans and competitors. It impresses fans and messes with the heads of foes. Meanwhile, behind the scenes, they are on top of every single detail about the preparation of the car, as well as studying data every free moment, sneaking looks at teammate data, practicing on the simulator, and racing with buddies "just for fun" in their shifter karts. But if you ever ask them about their level of preparation, the official fan club answer is a shrug of their shoulders and a wry smile.

Part One

Chapter 1

Pro Drivers as Coaches

Perhaps surprisingly, professional drivers are often lousy coaches. First, they usually hate riding with people, and second, many truly can't remember why they are fast! It's a funny thing, but when you do it for so long and have had every step in the process ingrained for what seems like your whole life, you really genuinely have trouble remembering what you do while you're driving. You see this in interviews sometimes when drivers are asked about some move or moment in the race, and they really have no recall of that defining moment, because it was all done subconsciously. These drivers start getting a bit paranoid after a while, and you can see it manifest in superstitions. Some top drivers are very superstitious.

That makes the whole driver training game quite tricky from the students' perspective, because the actual teaching ability of a driver has little to do with their track record. Make no mistake, you want a pro-level driver to teach you, even from day one, but they have to be as adept and accomplished at teaching as at driving to really be worth their sometimes very high daily rates. That means that while it's great to have your driving ingrained to a subconscious level (and we will spend a great deal of time on this very topic), you also need a driver/coach who maintains a high level of awareness during their driving so they can articulate what they do and relate that to what you are currently doing.

With my positions at the racing schools, I have been right in the middle of it all and have had a lot of experience with this for many years now. I've had to take these drivers. assess them on their teaching and driving ability, and design and facilitate instructor training sessions for them. Huge fun. Racing drivers are, if anything, really fun people. We realize we have been gifted a really lucky existence; yes, we'd rather be in an F1 car right now, but still, compared to most, this life is a dream come true.

So, how many pro drivers are there? Well, in the U.S. I have contact info for about 400 that also at least dabble in coaching. I would say 150 do it for a living to supplement their racing, and about 40 are really gifted drivers and teachers. Not coincidently, we are all pretty close friends off the track (but fierce competitors on the track). The two things that differentiate the good ones are caring about the individual student progressing and knowing what qualities and processes made them fast in the first place. Now, this may seem like an obvious trait of any good teacher in any field, but due to the ridiculously competitive, combative environment on and off the track, racecar drivers tend to be very self-centered, even slightly paranoid people, especially from the middle of the pro ranks, which is where most of us spend nearly our entire careers. Once they are on top, some manage to relax a little. The rest of the time you are fighting tooth and nail for the finite number of seats available. Not a very conducive environment for openness about one's technique. So, in most cases, racing drivers don't naturally make great instructors, which creates high demand for the few who are driving coaches.

This is all just basic human nature born out of the racing environment. In my travels as a coach, I have had the pleasure of dealing with many people from other industries, and they all behave exactly the same way (again, human nature being what it is); from Hollywood to military Special Forces to pro athletes to captains of industry, the same exact behavioral patterns emerge. If you think about it, the very (human) nature of competition does not have "sharing" very high up on the priorities list. In general, professional motorsports, while seemingly friendly on the outside, are nothing short of a fierce battleground in reality.

I'll be honest, most pro racers are driving instructors because they have no other way of making a living with their oddball skill set – maybe becoming a getaway driver is the other option? They are not instructors because they love to teach but because they have to teach to pay the bills. It is unfortunately just a job to those guys, and they obviously won't make good coaches. So, you might think on the other hand you could go with the super enthusiastic club racing and amateur racing driver/instructor. They are so happy to have the honor of being a club instructor and being thought of in that exalted light; the problem is the level of training is all over the map with these guys and is, at best usually just mediocre. The truth is, if they were really great drivers (and make no mistake, you want to be taught by a great driver); they would not be there in the first place, they would have naturally graduated into the pro ranks. I have probably made myself a bit unpopular with this paragraph, but the truth needs to see the light of day here. (Truth: It's kind of' the theme of the book!)

A question I hear quite a bit is, "Should I spend the money and go to a pro racing school or just go to a club school for initial training?" The thought is that you can get the initial stuff out of the way more cheaply with the club guys, get in some lapping days, maybe do a few club races to assess, and get your feet wet, THEN go to the pro school to refine your technique.

Let me be very clear here, those people are the worst, most difficult students at the pro school. In the perhaps short time they have been on the track, they have developed a pro+ level ego, along with more bad habits than you can ever hope to be rid of in a lifetime, let alone in the three days you have them at the pro school (even if they could put their ego aside). Again, this is not a slam at any well-meaning groups. This is the reality of my 20+ years of experience in the industry. The clubs can't really help it. They simply are victims of the natural order of things. Anytime a real talent emerges at the club level (and it does happen), they quickly want to see how they compare with the big boys and they head for pro racing. It's the natural order. That means that some very well-meaning, nice folks that have fun driving, racing, coaching, and creating a really nice environment are left behind. If you like, it's a little automotive Disneyland, a great place to spend a weekend with like-minded people who love a brand of car and using it on the track etc.

The club folk relative to the pro ranks remind me of the Olympics. You watch the opening ceremonies and see the countries proudly march into the stadium with their flags, and the differences are striking between the contingents from the large countries to those from the small. You have these tiny countries that show up with their basketball team, for example. Their most exalted national heroes, the best of the best in their tiny country.

In round one, due to the seeding, they face the U.S.A. and the Dream Team and get slaughtered. I mean, we all love an underdog, and in the Olympics, it can happen, and it's amazing when it does. I like "Cool Runnings" as much as the next person, but the reality is more predictable and tends to follow the natural order of things. The order of things and the empathy, precision, and nuance that is required to take a student on day one and move them forward, with the instructor able to read, react, and anticipate exactly what the student needs next, not too much and not too little, in a language they understand, with verbiage they can relate to. That is what it takes to make sure you, as a student are fully engaged in the process... Captivated is a good word. You will find the right people at a true pro school such as Jim Russell (now called Simraceway), Skip Barber, Bob Bondurant, etc. If you really ask around, you can also find independent professional coaches that meet the necessary strict criteria detailed above.

As an example, I was hired by some guys who had hired a much more accomplished and expensive driver as their dream celebrity coach before coming to me. They brought me in because this coach had crushed all of them by telling them that they were terrible and giving no instruction and/or coaching. He would actually take out the owner's manual to their cars and start reading them when they'd go out on the track to figure out if he wanted to buy one of their cars next (they all were quite wealthy and had very desirable cars), and then instead of feedback at the end of the session, he'd ask them about their cars! All of those guys were pretty darn good, by the way.

If, at the end of your journey, you end up club racing, that's fine. It feels plenty good being on the best team in a little country, but this book is not about that level; it is about striving for greatness. It is about sometimes having to be uncomfortably blunt with you because your time is precious. This field is hard enough without going down a wrong path or two because I wasn't brave enough to tell you the truth. It is a lifelong pursuit. I am not always a "great" driver, I am a quick driver, and I am a thoughtful, introspective driver/instructor. But, to consider myself consistently great would be flatly wrong! Oh, but make no mistake, I want it as badly as when I was a teenager. That carrot STILL dangles in front of me, tantalizingly close, and I pursue it with all my passion! I hope you feel the same way and therefore find benefit from my perspective and experience, even if it bruises the ego occasionally. Humility is the number one attribute of a successful student (or a successful teacher or person for that matter). Humility only gains us perspective, and gaining perspective only does one thing... It makes us wiser...It makes us crave wisdom.

So, what does wisdom gain you? The ability to see root causes, of problems. Fixing root causes and not just treating symptoms, is the basic cornerstone of teaching; and speaking of cornerstones, here is an example of how this really succeeds. One of the foundational driving skills to ingrain is that consistently driving fast is a game of anticipation, not reaction. You have to think and therefore look as far down the road as possible. The phrase "eyes up" (telling the student to look further down the road) is a great example; you hear it constantly at any school. Since most racers by design don't have great empathy, it doesn't occur to them that there are real ingrained reasons students don't do it right and repeat the mistake over and over (much to the instructors' and students' frustration, in many cases). It's not because the students don't understand or are not good enough; they actually physically can't make themselves look down the road. Why? It's because the teachers really can't teach, because they don't see the root cause of the issue. The root cause is so many steps away from the instruction "eyes up" that no student could possibly connect the dots and fix the issue. Efficient improvement starts with the root cause and only there; everything else is just a masked symptom, and that has never made anyone actually better.

The "low eyes" driver is that way for a reason; they are concerned about the present and therefore not planning for the future. So, you have to figure out why they are concerned: They are worried about the car in the corner... They are worried that they are near the physical limit of speed and the car may skid... They are worried that if the car skids, they won't be able to catch it. So, they aren't looking far enough down the road because they lack car control. That is the root problem. Car control is a learned skill, whether on the farm, in a snowy parking lot, in karts, or on a skid pad. If you never learn it, you will never be a driver that feels comfortable at the limit. The only way to make a driver without car control stop looking down and get their eyes up is to slow them down and get them to drive below their limit. The instant they do that, they regain cognitive bandwidth and now can plan. Therefore, telling them to look further down the road will never fix the problem; even if through sheer will power they force themselves to look further, they still don't have good car control, they were worried for good reasons, right!? Now they are ignoring the car control issue (though it is very real), and putting themselves (and everyone on the track with them) at risk. Not how it should be done.

Now that we've got that out of the way, I have great news for you! I have a system that is based on the reality of what you have read so far, not on a projection of who we like people to think we are. That's why this and only this will work. Oh, and tell your ego to relax... Doctor/patient privilege is in effect here. No one will know our many shared secrets! Everyone can still think you burst onto the scene as the second coming of Ayrton Senna. That's how every single great has done it and continues to do it.

Chapter 2

The Myth of the "Natural" Talent

Yes, I am saying natural talent is a myth. It appears to be real, but actually, when you dig into their history a bit, you may occasionally find they have never driven a race car before, but they have "driven" something. The love of speed starts really early in life. Even if you're in your "Autumn," I would venture that the itch you're scratching came from your childhood. Raise your hand if you ever did anything risky and dumb as a kid just for the thrill of it. OK, now everybody put your hands down! This is where the seed is planted, and some continue to do "risky dumb stuff" throughout their youth and (if they survive) refine and up the ante (careful not saying upping the risk, because their growing knowledge mitigates the risk increase at each step), and grow comfortable visualizing, planning, executing, analyzing, and refining. Then, one day they get a chance to jump in a kart or even a race car – and they fly. They come in and astonished observers ask the most magnificent question that their ego has had the pleasure of hearing: "You sure you've never driven one of these before!?!" May I present to you an amazing "natural" talent. Not everyone grew up in an environment that allowed this very useful experimentation that (while they thought they were just playing) gave them a balanced real feel for how they interact with the natural world and ingrained a process that will help them succeed at just about anything they tackle. You see, learning ability is the real talent.

There are other characteristics that differentiate people as well. It's not just as simple as you've either spent your childhood being a daredevil on a Big Wheel or a bike or not. Along with all that is the very real possibility that it went really wrong one day with that plywood ramp or rope swing and you got seriously hurt. Physically you've healed, but deep down the psychological scarring remains, and it has a real and negative effect on you at the exact moment you need clarity, not a triggered panic reflex. I have seen this countless times, and it is especially obvious with a student driving and me riding (on a skid pad usually) or when I am giving a hot lap. The instant the car slides, you see the panic attack; some get over it and gain some semblance of control a second or so later, some do not and simply can't. I would estimate half the population has the sort of trauma-triggered panic buried within that will affect their ability to ever do anything that is risky very well.

There is also the physiological response your body has to fear stimuli that is independent of the trauma you may or may not have had in your past. This is a large variable, and studies and my own experiences have shown that only 10% of the population has the proper "chemical cocktail" that is released during high risk situations to naturally have the ability to think clearly and not panic in "fight or flight" situations. This is a natural dispersion of these risk-taker genes that has always occurred in human beings. The 10% are the fighters who protect the village, the warriors (the opposite, ironically, of the "worriers"). The 90% think the 10% are crazy adrenaline junkies, and the 10% think the 90% are boring and live in fear. They are both right; relatively, the 10% have a lot more fun (kids that never grow up), but the 90% tend to be more pragmatic and therefore on the average live a lot longer. Funny enough, due to the influence of the nurture side on us, 90% of people think they are in the 10% and vice versa. There are infinite combinations of these traits, and they have a very large influence on how we learn and what strategy will work best for us.

Now, of course, you are wondering which one are you? Or actually, maybe you already have it pegged. Before we choose teams, you should know that both types have won World Championships (but their personal journeys are vastly different). So, here's the test: Do you literally laugh at fear? That's it, are you one of the "adrenaline junkies" who actually has a pleasant response to being scared? Does your "chemical cocktail" allow you to retain cognitive clarity (aka grace under pressure) at precisely those dangerous moments when you should panic, but don't panic? Do people think of you as brave? Remember, it's only 10% of the population (and it varies culturally and geographically). However, those 10% are drawn to these types of books and activities, so the crosscut of those of you reading is probably more up towards 50/50 and maybe more. Then again, real "fly by the seat of your pants" types don't like reading about doing stuff, they like doing stuff, and to heck with the instructions. We are, if anything, interesting.

So, what are the plusses and minuses of each type? It might seem like the "10 percenters" have all the advantages. Driving a race car without being scared – how ridiculously liberating, right!? Well yes, but that can be the issue, they tend to immediately be relatively fast, but (and you've guessed it by now) they tend to crash a lot. Crashing is expensive (so they better have deep pockets), oh, and it is risky, so they can get hurt (with physical, financial, and physiological trauma as a result). They get a great majority of the press and attention, so they also get most of the available sponsorship (but don't kid yourself... Still mostly self-funding along the way), but also need lots of second chances as they test everyone's patience hoping they "mature" before the money runs out or they have a career-ending crash.

The 90%, on the other hand, tend to be very methodical and analytical, much more concerned with everything because they have to take the time to rationalize and mitigate the risk along the way to progress. No "leaps of faith" here. Not very exciting, especially in the formative years, but they steadily grow and can end up being as fast (and seeming as "fearless") as anyone else. They have crashed a lot fewer cars along the way, but have had a hard time getting sponsorship, so they were probably self-funded for the long ride to the top (as a paid pro). Most don't have the financial wherewithal to make it to the top, and many more actually can't get over the fear to be able to be truly fast. In other words, it's tough for anyone, there is no defined and set path; we are all unique in our struggle for greatness.

Then there are the select few that become true greats. A level that somehow goes above what the very best that the 10% or 90% could ever achieve: What would that take? Obviously, it is incredibly rare. This is Bernt Rosemeyer, Tazio Nuvolari, Juan Manuel Fangio, Sterling Moss, Phil Hill, John Surtees, Jimmy Clark, Dan Gurney,

AJ Foyt, Mario Andretti, Jackie Stewart, Ayrton Senna, Alain Prost, Michael Shumacher, Sebastian Vettel, Lewis Hamilton, Sebastian Loeb, and, on a motorcycle, Valentino Rossi.

As you might imagine, true greats have somehow fully developed the positive traits of both the "brave" camp and the "methodical" camp, and become analytical adrenaline junkies. They started one way by nature but developed skills that were at first unnatural to them. They became complete drivers. They don't just climb out of the car, throw their helmet to the ground, and proclaim, "The car is sheet!" (A foreign accent really helps here!) And they never waste precious laps getting up to speed. They are confidently "on it" and hyper aware at all times in the car or in the paddock. The point is, no matter how good you become as a natural 10% or 90% driver, you can never be great without building step by agonizing step the same level of proficiency on the other side.

For example, let's say someone is the world's best 10% person but never developed the methodical thinking side. That would mean speed comes relatively easily, and therefore that person may not naturally be very hard-working in a relative sense. It's like someone who is good at visualizing math, so they can skip doing the homework and still get B's. They wouldn't develop the mindset to analyze and to learn the car so that they understand speed from the team engineer's perspective. They think the car's speed is not their problem; it becomes an unproductively polarized us vs. them atmosphere within their team. No one wins.

The real defining characteristic of a championship effort is efficient communication between the team engineers and the driver. You can buy the best car and have the best mechanics, engineers, and drivers, but if those entities that make up "a team" don't take action or communicate efficiently, then they simply will not be able to win consistently or perhaps at all. No joke, almost all pro teams, even up to F1, have some form of this dysfunction. It is everywhere. It takes humbleness, intelligence, patience, money, and a large dose of serendipity to put the magic combination together, yet if it is ever achieved, it is unstoppable because it is likely that they are the only team operating at that efficiency level in the entire paddock.

This holistic approach really works, whether you're a one-person operation club racing or auto crossing or driving F1. On every level of Motorsports, greatness can and does exist; this is a very reassuring truth. Don't worry, I'm not contradicting myself; it does occur in club racing, it just doesn't usually stay, as I earlier stated.

You might ask yourself, "Why doesn't every driver strive to become more complete?" This all seems like common sense, right? Well, again, it falls back to human nature. We don't really associate being more complete with the goal, we strive to be better. They are two distinct paradigms. Let me explain...

It comes from us and other people throughout our lives trying to continuously categorize us. We end up telling ourselves, "I'm good at this" and "I'm not very good at that" throughout our whole lives. We usually do this quite superficially without much real analysis. Think... A whole life of this.

A fun aside to this is how wrong we can be about our REAL strengths and weaknesses: We don't really think about all the reasons this "thing" rubbed us the wrong way. An easy example could be from school: You might be the next Albert Einstein, but, because you had a string of bad teachers in math and physics, you never developed that love for something that, unbeknownst to you, you could have been brilliant at. You'll go your whole life intentionally avoiding anything that even mildly sounds anything like science, always steering away from it. If anyone asks, you genuinely believe you're not good at it, and as you say that you believe that, you make it true (perception is reality)... And you're completely wrong.

We end up with two columns: Stuff we think we're good at and stuff we think we're not good at. It's not quite as black and white as that, but for the sake of making a point, let's pretend it's absolute. So, we have two lists, and what our ego does next is discard/bury the negative list so we can feel good about ourselves. Now we want to make ourselves "better"; what do you think we work on? We should go straight to the top of our weakness list, but we don't – we can't even find it! Instead, we go straight to our strengths, making us even more out of balance as a driver. We hate dealing with our weaknesses and would rather spend time hanging out where our fragile precious egos are happy (stay positive right?)...keep building those strengths and watch how you plateau as a driver no matter how hard you try. This relates to what I mentioned earlier as a warning about how we naturally filter what we are learning to emphasize what our egos find acceptable. All of it done without a single conscious thought.

We all have to work if we want to be great, and working hard and having gritty determination means we are willing to charge at full speed headfirst at our grimmest, most buried fears. If we spend our time focused on eradicating weaknesses, we get amazing efficient return on our time. If we keep hammering at our strengths, we only eke out tiny gains, due to the law of diminishing returns. We think that's it for us, we've reached our potential because we've gone as far as we can with our strengths and developed our best possible work-around for our weaknesses... That's as good as we can ever be, right? Do you see how flawed our natural logic is?

You see, "great" driving is not consistently sustainable, just like great anything else. Everybody has slumps due to the complexity of greatness. You are dealing with so many factors, from team dynamics to how good the car is that year to your own house being in order. Each of these items individually is fantastically complex on its own; having them all in order is rare, but when you manage to align them... Wow. The drivers listed above managed to consistently slip into greatness, which takes amazing composure and complete dedication. They are the type of people who would excel at anything they had tried, because they had nailed down the process of greatness to such an extent that it all became second nature to them; then the puzzle was solved, the mystery revealed.

This magical alignment has been studied for millennia and is interwoven into every culture. In an exaggerated form, it is even a part of popular culture in many movies, such as the *Star Wars* and *The Matrix* franchises. Unfortunately, it has typically been brushed aside by our increasingly superficial cultures that cannot comprehend the endless possibilities and depth hidden within all of us... It is simply known as flow. Flow is us at our very best, when we are free from any outside distractions, confident and stress-free, transcendent, living in the moment but simultaneously flowing into the future.

We all have experienced flow moments, more often as children, due to our uncanny ability as we grow up to slowly strangle our own potential in a silly attempt to avoid anything that can be interpreted as weakness. As children, we were free to experiment and explore our worlds, and due to the simplicity of our very nature, we experienced euphoria (slipping into flow state) quite often and quite easily. Flow is the ultimate happy place; it is us at our very best.

My moments of flow as a child were, probably like yours, too numerous to count; I had unlimited access to creating flow-inducing scenarios (just as we all did). My version had woods, with trees, rocks, ponds, streams, and hillsides. It also had paths, sidewalks, and roads, plus abandoned lots and buildings. I was provided (nearly every Christmas and birthday) with tools of pure flow-inducing enjoyment: Big Wheels, bikes, skateboards, skis, roller blades, dirt bikes, minibikes, and go-karts. All of this was guided by the inspiration of our limitless imaginations – and frankly, a keen desire to one-up my friends.

I still, to this day, take great pride in doing something well the first time I try it. I have learned what this skill is, now that I have witnessed it so often in students. It is the art of visualization, aka practical daydreaming. My friends and I would sit on our bikes pondering a new potential jump (off a building wall or a dirt pile that, if you hit it just hard enough, you just might clear a fence, for example), every one of us wanting to be the first to clear it; you would have instant hero status, building a reputation that could span neighborhoods... You would have real hard-earned respect. We all wanted it. There were predictable patterns that emerged within our group. We had a guy that wanted to be first so badly that he would just hurtle himself at anything without any forethought, and he always crashed and burned, much to the sidesplitting amusement of all his "concerned" friends. He would dust himself off and mope back to the group. We needed that guy, he provided us with valuable data. The guys that usually cleared it would never go first; they would sit back and analyze. They would visualize the jump over and over; drawing out similarities from previous jumps and adding data from jump attempts as they occurred. Then suddenly it would click in their heads and they would go... Hopefully before the others figured it out. I was often that guy. I knew the visualization was the key, and I needed to be faster and more accurate than my buddies to beat them to the glory.

I have continuously refined that same technique throughout my life; it is my single most developed and valuable skill. It enables anything good I have ever done, and combined with refinement (practice), it has given me highly addictive moments of relative greatness.

What does potential driving greatness have to do with flow, you might ask? Remember, flow is us completely immersed in the moment without stress, so comfortable in the moment that we are actually very nearly time traveling by vividly visualizing the future. We're not just sitting on the run-up to some new jump visualizing go or no go, we are in the air and completely comfortable, picturing the landing with such detail that we are completely confident in the outcome. This is why flow flows, it is a foundational concept to wrap your head around. I cannot hope to be great or even smooth living just in the present; the present is too fleeting to do anything about it, but the future is unwritten, so that's where I must focus. I must continuously smoothly transition the present into the future to enable flow to occur. How far ahead can you think? That, too, is unlimited. I want a student to at least be able to think a turn ahead, but real high- level flow is far, far beyond that.

Perhaps the greatest tangible example for any of you that doubt flow's existence or are having a hard time feeling what it means is rallying. Hopefully you have seen many in-car videos from pro rallying; if not, hit pause on the book now and head to YouTube. The evidence of flow exists in all the amazing stages that are online these days. It is the timing of the navigator's pace notes that give it all away, have you ever noticed? They are not telling the driver about the corner they are in (it's obviously too late for that to help). They are calling out usually two to three corners ahead at a rate that allows the driver to process, refine, tie together, and optimize every successive corner or obstacle in their path. If done well, it's a single flowing connection between the co-driver and driver, and that's why switching co-drivers is rarely done once that bond has formed, which is really cool, when you think about it.

Looking back on my flow-filled childhood, it's funny now to reminisce and think of all my absurd explanations to friends and family for all of the scrapes, bruises, and, of course, destroyed stuff and clothing. I'd be getting a reprimand from my parents and agreeing to "never try anything like that again," while meanwhile actually simultaneously devising my even more daring follow-up. I had a bike frame that was welded so often by the local radiator shop that I was on a first-name basis with everyone there. I could walk straight back into the shop area (bypassing the regular customer storefront) with what now looked like a caricature of a bike and have my frame re-welded on the spot for just the cost of materials.

So, to add it all up, we are trying to be great; greatness is fleeting and directly tied to flow state. Flow state is not something that can be forced; we slip into it when every variable involved in our activity is comfortably accounted for. You can consciously try to tell yourself that everything is fine, but your subconscious actually triggers flow, and it cannot be lied to. Flow will not happen unless every box has been ticked, no exceptions. So, when we don't flow, we are under the power of greatness's greatest foe: Fear.

Chapter 3

Fear Factor
(the killer of flow)

Fear is a powerful thing in anyone's life, but getting someone to admit or even realize that... Good luck, right? It is absolutely not something we are willing to talk about, and it's on the top of the uncool topic list (especially us ego-driven guys; the ladies have an advantage here). We are OK talking about "confidence" with the team; that is the accepted term! Whether we are willing to acknowledge it or call it what it is, it is a major player in our lives. We often call it stress, but stress itself is simply unresolved fear. If you really think about it, fear in some way, shape, or form influences every decision we make. Should I eat this? (It will make me fat.) Should I ask them out? (They may say no.) Should I buy that expensive something? (I could lose my job, and then what?) It goes on and on – from small decisions to huge ones, fear is there with you in lockstep, "guiding" you in its quest to keep you alive and unfortunately average at best. The big problem with us is that most fear is irrational, and irrational fear only holds us back – it has no positive contribution to our lives. Irrational fear is presumed danger or limits, not actual limits and dangers. In our normal lives, the type of fear that is influencing us typically goes unnoticed; but when you are trying to push your boundaries and test limits, it boxes us in, stifling our potential. We are indeed our own worst enemies. Like most things, if fear were always rational, it would be only a good productive thing, but it's seldom just rational. Let's take a look at fear and how it applies to driving, since it is a major player in anyone's ability to perform at any level.

Thinking in extremes: The completely fearless driver is a dangerous one, but the irrationally fearful driver is also just as dangerous. The rational driver, of course, strikes just the right balance – does this seem to be a theme here?! It is hard, though, to separate the rational from the irrational until you have the experience to do so. Think of irrational fear as your best guess. A relevant racing example is what you will experience if you are ever lucky enough to drive a real high downforce car, a prototype, or a middle to upper tier formula car. The cars have a very dynamic maximum G-force. In a hairpin, they behave like any other racecar (heck, they are probably slower than a good shifter kart); BUT, as you pass 80 mph or so (of course depending on the car) and get above 100, 120, or 140 through a corner, they are developing more and more downforce. This is very hard to comprehend when you're in the car; you want to corner at 120 at the same grip level as through the hairpin. It might sound silly here, but when you're in the car, anything else seems, well, ridiculously foolish. You stay out for the whole session trying to dip your toe in the murky waters of invisible downforce; you were told beforehand it could do it and you promised to try, but now you're in the car, and it just seems crazy to trust this thing you can't see. This is irrational fear. The physics are real, you comprehend and believe in the science when you're not in the car, but right there in the moment Hell no! It takes experience to actually dare to dip that toe in the water, and what happens after a while is that you eventually realize that the car, for example, can corner three times harder through a high-speed corner than a low speed one, and brake four times harder at speed (which we'll talk in detail about in the downforce chapter).

Think about the general public and its irrational fear that if you corner hard enough, a car will flip over (if I had a nickel for every time a student asked me that in all seriousness). Why this irrational fear? The answer is Hollywood and the "Cannon Roll." In the movie *Casino Royale*, an Aston Martin rolls on a wet road, which is simply impossible in the real world. How is it done? High explosives and an 18" chunk of telephone pole fired out of the bottom of the car. In a high-budget film, the pole is CGI-ed out; in low budget movies, you can usually see it somewhere in the debris created by the disintegrating car. The average person has probably seen hundreds of cannon rolls on TV or at the theater, and if you don't realize there's movie magic at work, you believe (irrationally) that cars roll over. You have to realize that this actually causes very real crashes in the real world. I have had countless people tell me after the fact that they were afraid to steer in an emergency because they thought their car would roll. It is the single most common question at any entry-level school.

The funny thing about fear is how temporary it is, if confronted because once you have learned a task, no matter how scary it initially was, the moment you really understood how to complete the task, the fear was gone. You rationalized it into non-existence and are now left with only the real rational fear, what we would call a respect for the task. A horror movie is an obvious example; once you have seen it and know exactly where the chain saw swings into frame, the "fun" is gone, right?

Remember the downforce example; getting in the car, we knew it would stick, but once out there, no way. What seems easy when we are feeling nice and rational outside the car rears its scary monstrous head when we're actually trying it. We are, in fact initially two completely different people, one who is amazingly rational when there is no perceived risk, and another who can be quite irrational when under pressure. This is embarrassing, we don't like talking about it or admitting it to anyone. We'd rather suffer in silence... That damn ego again. Just remember you're just being human. The goal, of course, is to just slip into the car and drive it right at the limit as calmly as you're sitting there right now sipping your latte reading this. A fraction of the people who try actually achieve this level of grace under pressure. It is a (worthy) lifetime pursuit; only good can come from any gains made on this.

Out of the thousands I have coached for a few hours and the hundred or so I have coached for days, I can think of a few students who were obsessively determined to the point that they reached that level. How did I know? When I asked them to incorporate something additional, they would immediately implement it; and you could see them fiddling only with that one task, automatically adjusting the other parameters to make it fit. It is a beautifully efficient thing to behold, and they make progress so quickly that I am soon made proudly redundant (since my job is done).

Part Two

Chapter 4

Getting in the Optimal Drive Zone

Commonly referred to as "The Zone," this flow level occurs when all the tasks of driving that car at the limit that day can be handled with zero conscious input. That means you have enough subconscious range in each of the necessary tasks to handle everything thrown at you that day. It is an amazing achievement anytime it occurs, considering the complexity of the task and the environment in which it occurs. Rarely achieved, often attempted... Greatness.

If it all seems out of reach, realize you have achieved this before, heck, probably in several disciplines, just perhaps not in something so complex and dangerous and perhaps not in a while. That should inspire you to try for greatness; you have it within you, you just need to break down and learn all the facets of this complicated endeavor with true honesty and dedication. It is all laid out here... Something amazing is waiting for you on the other side.

Flow state works like this: First, you are handling everything subconsciously, so what does that take exactly? You have to have the tasks nailed down to such an extent that you can deal with the tasks and the normal variations of the tasks without any conscious intervention required. Think of running up a flight of stairs. You can do it without any conscious thought, even though you're not placing your feet exactly the same for each step; and each step is subtly different, but it's all still within a range you would consider "normal", thus no conscious thought is required. What if a step is "out of range" though? We've all done this - how about walking up the stairs at night in your house when you think there is one more or one less step than there actually is! Comedy ensues; now your conscious mind is fully involved with dealing with the "catch" (correction) that hopefully happens. It's no different in the car; things are normal if we can subconsciously deal with the fix. Little bit of understeer/oversteer, slightly off line, etc.? All OK, no alarms. Any surprises invoke conscious thought and, hopefully, correction, but we snap out of flow.

We are phenomenal subconscious multitaskers, but we absolutely cannot consciously multitask. That is another total myth. That's why great only exists while in flow state. If we are out of subconscious range and consciously fixing something, our whole game is thrown off while we deal with the problem. That pass you were trying to execute? Not happening. That corner you were just beautifully carving through?" Gone; you're now off line. That braking point? You just missed it. We are organic supercomputers, until one little insignificant synapse fires off a bad command and we get the equivalent of a screen freeze right in the middle of something... well... quite important. It's no coincidence that the usual cause of most plane crashes is pilot error; what causes the pilot to make the critical mistake is having more than one problem at a time to deal with. It not only snaps us out of flow, but makes us prone to critical mistakes in high stress situations.

Why did the screen freeze? There was a flaw in the programming of one of our tasks. Something surprised us. We need to get back in there and incorporate the new learning into the flawed task (that's what mistakes are good for, right? That, and to keep us humble), so that our "normal range" now incorporates the new information.

Taking the computer analogy a step further (and to endear myself to the sim jockeys reading), think of your subconscious as computer RAM. Very fast, right? You want all your driving tasks loaded into your RAM while you're driving. An out-of-range mistake or a surprise is your RAM having to access your much slower hard drive (let's assume it's not an SSD), and you get a frame rate drop or a screen freeze. The cool thing is that our organic supercomputers have unlimited RAM, unlike our pathetic silicon-based replicas. We can ingrain skills endlessly, and we can adjust our subconscious continuously. The more you learn, the larger your normal window gets for each task and the easier it is for you to remain in flow; you simply get surprised less.

So, what is our role? Simply put, we balance the car and we aim the car.

It is how we blend braking and acceleration's longitudinal g-force into the cornering car's lateral g-force that distinguishes the ham-fisted driver from the virtuoso. It is amazing to think of how much time, money, and resources have been spent trying to explain this simple truth. We balance the car. The other task is aiming the car, and we only need some simple geometry for that one.

So, to summarize: put the car on a more efficient path and balance it better than the other guy's, and if its holds together, you'll beat them every time, and you will have achieved relative greatness.

Seems so simple, right? So why, then, are so few really great at it? It's just some simple math and off you go to grab some World Championship glory.

It's the whole human being thing that gets in the way, dynamic vs. static analysis; what seems relatively easy when sitting still is a whole lot more complex and therefore difficult in motion.

It's the environment in which you're doing your "simple math" that's the issue... The environment can kill you, and you don't let yourself forget it. The fear gets in the way and it is rational fear, there is real risk!

Psychology is a complex topic even in a static state; throw in the life-threatening environment and things get exponentially more complex. The world's armies have been dealing with this for millennia.

How do you get a soldier to stop being so distracted by the din of war that he can remember and therefore execute his orders in the heat of battle?

The answer, of course, is training, and training is only successfully done one way for humans. You break everything down into individual elements and teach them in a logical order from the beginning. Once each skill is ingrained, you add another skill. You constantly test them in ever more complex scenarios, that build in the new skill just after the trainees have ingrained them, until you have completed every individual skill. In the end, you have a soldier. Through repetition and progressive challenges, after the program, they thoroughly understand things they could not even imagine a relatively short time before.

The training, as mentioned, must be logical and absolutely realistic from the budding soldiers' perspective. If done properly, there is no doubt they are fully prepared to handle what were previously daunting tasks in their near future.

You create grace under pressure... Think about it... You create grace under pressure. Most would say that you either have it or you don't. They either don't want to make the effort or simply can't imagine doing the work to create grace under pressure, so they live with what they have and assume it's all cast in stone, rigid, and unmoving, and are limited their whole lives to mediocrity.

So, are you willing to go there? To do the work? OK then, how do you create or nurture something so fundamental, that is so buried within us? Unfortunately, we must commit to do things most of us rightly hate and avoid every single time that we can wriggle out of it. We have to be bluntly honest with ourselves, and there is nothing comfortable about that. This is where we, along with most driving books, go wrong: We base our starting point on layer upon layer of work-arounds and coping mechanisms. You are probably now wondering what the heck I am on about now... It's a fundamental scientific truth that if what you know/assume/think about your driving ability this instant is not 100% accurate, then the whole process will be flawed going forward. You cannot take what you currently know about driving and use that as your baseline. No matter how much you try to correct as you go, all your "data" about your knowledge is flawed. Just like the soldier, you need to be torn down and rebuilt correctly from your very essence if you want to be the greatest and best version of you possible. Trust me, you are not honest with yourself about your driving and most things in your life. I am not talking down to you; I am the same. We are for better or for worse, human. We neatly call these mistruths "coping mechanisms"; they really help when something goes wrong and we can't figure out why... They provide a kind of closure and allow us to move on from unpleasantness. If we took the time to really sort everything out, we'd never get anywhere, right? Coping mechanisms and work-arounds are just fine, if you don't care about excelling at something, but since you're reading this, I'm going to assume that is not the case with you.

So, as you are sitting there now reading this (just as I am writing this), you are a combination of some measure of absolute truth and a large measure of stuff we have convinced ourselves is the truth. This is normal and human, but it certainly is not very real or productive, if our greatest self is the goal. A good way to start is to have a completely open mind, with ego set well aside. Assume all you have learned thus far is probably somewhat flawed, and then be pleasantly surprised when some of it is actually quite good already. You must analyze everything, searching for anything out of line; if you miss or ignore just one fundamental flaw, you will unfortunately never achieve greatness. You have been warned.

So, we start a lifelong journey together right now, because I now have you humble and honest and hopefully eager... Exactly the state of mind in which to move forward.

Wait, did I just say "lifetime" a moment ago!? Why does this take so long and therefore require such discipline?

Well, it is because we can only learn things one at a time, because conscious multitasking, as mentioned, is a complete myth. We can only truly focus on one thing at a time. We are trying to very carefully ingrain many processes in a certain order, one at a time. You are only potentially good at things you have ingrained properly. It's like writing computer code; it needs to be written exactly right, line by painstaking line, or we're going to get error messages or worse. It's bad enough on our computers, but who wants to be mentally hitting Control-Alt-Delete in the middle of a 140 mph corner? ...yikes. So, we must be very accurate and methodical in how we put the information into ourselves. We have to respect the realities of how we really learn and push that pesky ego out of the equation. We can only learn things one at a time because we can only consciously do one thing at a time. It takes multiple conscious repetitions to ingrain something. Again, I have seen this so many times, I don't need to quote some third-party study – I have lived this. Be patient with yourself, and be honest and methodical... Be 100% sure before you move on.

As I previously established in my "low eyes" example, it all starts with good car control, and there is no better place to start car control training than on a skid pad.

SKID PAD

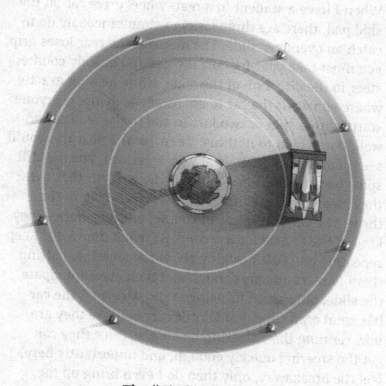

The "Circle of Trust"

I love the skid pad, that simple little circle with ample run off... I have learned so much about people and, therefore, myself on that silly little circle. (Maybe I'll get "Blipshift" to print me an "Everything meaningful I have ever learned about life was shown to me riding on a skid pad" tee shirt.) It is difficult to be a passenger on a skid pad all day; you have to constantly deal with potential motion sickness, but I love it, in spite of its "vomit comet" status.

When I have a student in a rear-wheel drive car on the skid pad, there are three tasks to simultaneously do to catch an oversteer slide. The moment the rear loses grip, you must take your foot off the gas and quickly counter steer in the direction of the slide, while looking exactly where you want the car to go. After the demo, everyone starts with a spin or two just to add to the realities of, well, doing next to nothing. Then, on the next try, you'll see them try one (almost always steering). The car still spins because they didn't lift off the gas, but that's OK; they have taken the first small step with ONE of the three. The car still spins, of course, but they notice they kind of had it held for a second. So, what do we do? Keep repeating and ONLY talking about the steering, getting them to react quickly enough and then even anticipate the slide, only again focusing on the steering; the car has spun each time, but I don't care because they are now refining their steering technique. Once they can get the steering quickly enough, and importantly here, feel the breakaway, only then do I even bring up the throttle lift. In fact, when I mention it for the first time, very often I get the response, "I thought I was lifting my foot off the gas." They are not even aware they are staying on it because they are so intently focused on getting the steering right. We then progress through the throttle (people absolutely hate lifting off the throttle for oversteer), then finally bring up where they are looking to complete the three skills. Now they are doing them all together, and of course we are no longer spinning and the recoveries are getting smoother and smoother. When do I know they have it? I do something to occupy their conscious mind by asking them an off-the-topic question just before the slide starts, like "Think it's going to rain today?" If they still catch the slide as well as answering the question, catching this particular oversteer slide is ingrained... They have now earned some drifting practice (which everyone rightly loves!)

So, this is how we learn, one piece of the puzzle at a time, and this puzzle has many, many pieces. We must respect the process. There are NO SHORTCUTS. People hate this, too; I have had mega rich students ask, "Can I buy shortcuts!?", and the mega talented from another sport tell me, "I already know this stuff." Yes, you understand a process in your career, but you don't yet understand this process and this tool. You must respect the process and the time it takes each step of the way. Everyone must go through this.

The trouble starts when we expect this stuff to be easy (like learning kung fu in the movie *The Matrix*) and get frustrated because others may be able to ingrain things quicker. This often leads to frustration and people quitting the sport. We all learn at different rates, because, as we've discussed, we are all very different. It is not just talent that makes you fast, and you can think of talent as your rate of learning, realistically. It is also your determination. Always remember you can be just as good as "the natural" driver; you are just going to have to be more determined than they are to get to the same place. Then remember that this extra determination will actually make you a stronger driver and racer than "the natural" at the same level of driving. That has always been the silver lining for the people who have really had to earn it... They grow up tougher, and that is not to be underestimated.

Are you serious about this? Do you really want to be your very best? This could be embarrassing; you will probably get worse at several steps along the way (since part of progressing is temporarily regressing). It will be awkward, your friends may wonder what happened to you, but if you take this crucial first step and start with only the real truth, you will be shocked at how good (and maybe great) you can really be.

Just a reminder: Driving well is unnatural. No one has ever been naturally great...

Car control is the foundational skill. As long as you are still driving, you should be improving your car control, taking it to higher and higher and more granular levels. Car control is simply the driver's ability to manage slides or skids, but as previously mentioned, that skill set is a primary enabler of flow. For the sake of clarity, I use the term "slide" for something the driver intended to happen and the term "skid" for something the driver did not intend to happen. Why the distinction? Both are very real, but only one is scary, and it occurs when you have exceeded the limit of the car but weren't aware you were near the limit (so it is a surprise). There are three types, two of which are well known and a third one that is almost mythical. The two well-known types mean the driver has made a mistake and needs to fix it, and the third just to smile and enjoy the ride. Of course, I am referring to understeer and oversteer as the well-known first two types, and the four-wheel drift as the third (driving Nirvana).

So how is sliding or skidding defined? The normal way of describing them is to talk about slip angle, which is the direction the tire is actually going vs. the direction the rim holding the tire is pointing. We will spend a whole chapter on tires so you can really understand them. Since all driving technique comes from them, I think you'll agree they're worth at least that!

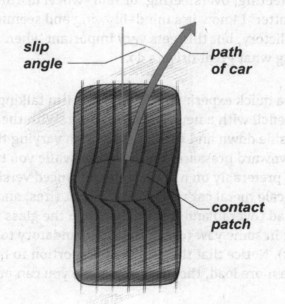

In engineering texts, you'll read that if the rear slip angle is greater than the front slip angle, then you are oversteering, and, conversely, if front exceeds rear, then you are understeering. You have to think in terms of an airplane for a moment and get acquainted with the term "yaw". Slip angle is the tire's direction of travel vs. the rim, and yaw is the same thing; but yaw refers to the lateral motion of the car itself (or aircraft) vs. the direction it's pointed. The rate of turn is conveniently called the "yaw rate." If you know the radius of a corner, you can predict the correct yaw rate to get through the corner that will keep you either exactly on that radius, or oversteering tighter to the inside or understeering wide off it. What's interesting about the definitions of understeer and oversteer is that technically the car doesn't need to actually be sliding or skidding to be understeering, oversteering, or four-wheel drifting, for that matter! I know it's mind-blowing and seemingly contradictory, but this gets very important when defining what great drivers do.

Here's a quick experiment to see what I'm talking about: Get a pencil with a new-ish eraser on it. With the pencil eraser side down and vertical, play with varying the load (or downward pressure) on the eraser while you twist the eraser, preferably on a glass table. Advanced version: Get a 1:18 scale metal car model with rubber tires, and play with load (overall and front to back) on the glass table, mixing in some yaw (car noises are mandatory to make it work). Notice that the grip is in proportion to the load, and the more load, the more slip angle you can produce.

STATIC CAR

The baseline: a car either sitting still or moving (but not accelerating or braking) on level ground.

BRAKE DIVE

*load transfer
rear to front*

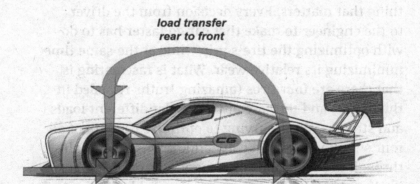

When decelerating, grip is added to the front as it proportionally is removed from the rear

ACCELERATION SQUAT

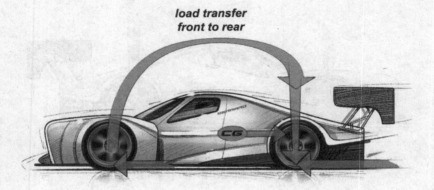

*load transfer
front to rear*

During acceleration, grip heads to the rear as it is transferred from the front

So, this tire thing is important; it is simply the only thing that matters. Every decision from the driver to the engineer to make that car go faster has to do with optimizing the tire's grip while at the same time minimizing its relative wear. What is fascinating is that there are four tires (amazing truths revealed in this book!) and they are always under different loads and stresses. We are trying to optimize the grip of all four simultaneously in a dynamic environment, all through the thousands of components of the vehicle itself and balanced by the biggest variable of all... A human being. Also consider the surface of the track; it is always changing with the vehicle's interaction and the atmospheric variables. It's simply amazing that we have ever made a full lap!

What we are trying to achieve is near peak slip angle at all times from all four tires; whoever gets closest is the fastest. There it is in black and white, the secret is out. Now everyone can be fast.

So, what is "peak slip angle"? It is determined partially by the tire manufacturer: It is the sum hysteresis (elastic twist) of the contact patch before it can't hold on any longer. The other very relevant and cool variable, as you saw in the experiment, is that the peak slip angle varies with load. All driving technique is derived from these two truths; that is why drivers, even the ones who don't care at all about engineering, have to have a good working knowledge of tires just to be good, let alone great. Some may chime in that they don't consciously know anything about tires, but luckily for them, their subconscious saves the day every time – they just haven't ever really thought about why they have the great feel they have.

There are lots of tire books and software out there for engineers, and they feature many impressive equations. We fortunately don't need to be too bothered with the math, but we do need a reasonably deep understanding and relationship with the tires under any car we happen to be driving. To ignore the tires and how to optimize them is to drive blind. You might consider the car to be a more important focus, but you'd be wrong. The vehicle should be set up for the tires, not for the driver; the entire vehicle is simply the middleman between you and the contact patches. The contact patch is king, and you have four tires, and at any given moment they need slightly different things. It's your job to be efficient with them, to extract balanced maximum grip from all four simultaneously, and to do it with minimum stress to the tires. So, what is it about these mysterious round black things?

First of all, tires are shockingly complex to produce, and the options and variations possible in their design and manufacturing are frankly staggering. I didn't always appreciate this complexity. I was lucky enough to start working with Michelin in the late 90's, and the whole crazy world of tires really opened my eyes forever. Learning how critical they are and, as a driver, how to manage them properly has by far the greatest effect on your potential success.

The second thing to really consider is that tires are, as mentioned, load-sensitive. The amount of grip they produce is proportional to the load that is placed on them (hopefully you played around with the pencil eraser or model car earlier). Realize without this reality, the whole "we balance the car" thing would vanish and everyone would just nudge up to the limit and hold there, because you wouldn't be able to manipulate grip. OK, now realize that that's exactly how most average track drivers drive. If they want to change the balance of the vehicle, they actually physically change the vehicle's set-up. Don't worry, we'll mess around with set-up as well, but we always first see if we can adjust the balance dynamically while driving.

The next thing to realize is that tires are, of course, elastic. We know load affects grip, so now imagine that sometimes thousands of pounds of load transferred through the vehicle with all of its solid bushings and stoutly built components, not a bit of give or play anywhere... Then it hits the tire and of course the tire is rolling, using friction created by is contact patch adhering to the surface. It's full of air (OK, often nitrogen) and made of rubber, which is very different than the unforgiving nature of the rest of the car. At least on a car we have a suspension to add some compliance along with that tortured tire; think of a racing kart where the tire is 90% of the compliance in the kart (that has no suspension other than some well-tuned chassis flex).

The tire puts up with a lot. It's no wonder they are a "consumable" and a major line item for teams big or small. They are also responsible for communicating with us, giving constant feedback as to how close they are to the limit (under or over). They do that in a few ways, and a combination of a couple of those felt or heard simultaneously give us an exact picture of how all four are doing at any given moment. We talked about slip angle earlier - what it is and how it happens. It can be a twisted contact patch due to cornering, or a pulled or pushed contact patch due to acceleration or braking; and, of course, it could be a combined twist and pull, or twist and push, as we are blending controls. This force through the tire also changes the forces through the steering wheel; how the front contact patches are loaded and where they are located changes steering effort. You learn to read this; it gives you real-time vital information on how good a job you are doing of optimizing the front tires. The rear tires you sense more with your inner ear; and as for yaw, we are very sensitive to yaw or rotation of the car, especially if we are very well belted in. When you put the two together, we have a live hardwired connection to each contact patch. We spoke earlier about the importance of visualization. After working with tires and race cars for so long, I can't help but actually visualize the contact patches while I am driving. I use it to finely adjust the balance and to help me visualize set-up changes I'd like to try with the car. Bottom line: The more connected with the tire you can be, the better racer you will become.

The last important consideration about tires is that their characteristics are different-things like how they like to be warmed up, when they peak (grip wise), and how quickly the grip tapers over time. Then there is pressure, temperature range, how much camber they like, and on and on. Spend time with on-site tire engineers, do your homework, be methodical when learning a new tire, and be very sensitive to the process each particular tire demands for peak performance.

If you stop to think about it, what we do is set the racecar up around the tires' characteristics, then we drive dynamically, chasing ideal balance for as much of every lap as possible for the life of those tires. Dynamically chasing ideal balance is really what we do, foot by foot, turn by turn, and lap by lap. It is all to serve the really important bit of the package-not the car, not the driver, but the humble tire.

The great car balancer gets another few percentage points of grip out of the car because instead of just driving to an understeer or oversteer grip "limit", they adjust the balance of the car on the fly to now make the limit a slightly higher/faster "four-wheel drift" that's not necessarily a sliding drift, because we're talking about manipulating the slip angles before the tire slides. This results in a reduction of steering I call ZEROSTEER.

These adjustments the driver is making are, of course, the manipulation of three controls: the steering, the brake, and the accelerator. The blending of these controls is where the magic happens (or doesn't), how the driver releases the brake and where, relative to steering input, speed and location, then through and on to the exit where the throttle is applied somewhere after the brake release at the optimal rate relative to the steering being removed.

There is an art to all this, and as in the study of any art, you start to see patterns. One important pattern to notice is that better drivers steer less; this is a generalization, but it is very true and equally very important. We talked about the simple geometry of the path through the corner as one of our primary responsibilities, so that is a set specific arc we have prescribed the car to follow that has a steering angle associated with it. It should be simple and done, right? It isn't though. Why, you may ask? Because of the already discussed elastic property of tires: Slip angle, which is determined by vehicle balance. We set that, of course. If the car has too much rear grip relative to front, the car will require more steering angle to follow the prescribed path and will be prone to understeer. If the front conversely has too much grip, then the rear will be likely to slide before the front and require counter steering if not immediately corrected. Picture that for a moment in slow motion. We enter the turn with a little too much trail brake (releasing the brake slowly after we've turned in) and perhaps one mph of excessive speed. The extra speed requires a bit of extra brake, and that, combined with that ideal geometric line, is asking just a bit more overall grip from the car than it has available. Now, since we are necessarily braking a bit too hard to get rid of extra speed (and to hopefully still make the apex,) the grip of the car is slightly more to the front than the rear than is ideal. Using our mind's eye in super slow motion, picture the rear tire (for visualization, the outside rear tire-it's carrying most of the rear load) twisting under building cornering forces, then upon reaching its max slip angle, breaking free and starting to slide. Now pause; think about what's now happening in the cockpit with the driver. They have already initiated the turn-in and are in the process of pointing the car at the apex, so there is some steering angle inputted into the car, right? OK, so as the rear steps out, the driver should be immediately reducing steering to catch the soon-to-be-sliding rear. If they are quick about it, they can easily catch this excess yaw without having to go past center with the wheel and without using "counter steer." Let that sink in deeply. If caught quickly enough, that little extra rear slip angle allowed them to reduce steering. Now dig a little deeper, and make the focus of our little visualization on just before the slide actually happened; we are doing the same thing as a driver, but we are gently and proportionally reducing the steering, due to the rear slip angle building faster than the front. Remember, slip angle feels like sliding, but it's actually the elastic twist between the contact patch and the rim. So, if you generate more rear slip angle than front slip angle, you will get through the corner with less steering and you will be faster. Now I am speaking very generally here, because there are significant variables, including the actual tires' characteristics, the vehicle, and the actual corner radius – BUT the principal is sound. This is what great drivers do.

So, what do we do with that information? From my example, we can now say we didn't enter to corner too fast. Using slip angle, we can finesse the car into and through a corner faster. It is the granular ability to manipulate balance that separates the good from the great. It's picking up a few tenths of a mile an hour that adds up to a whole second of difference in time on an average two-mile track. The typical lap time difference between pro drivers in the same car on the same given day is usually under two tenths of a second(!). Imagine how subtle that feel advantage is! The goal is always to carry more speed than the other guys while wearing your tires the same (if not better); that is 100% done by balancing the car better than they do. Now there is a car set-up side to this as well that optimizes things, and we will discuss that in detail; but given the same car, optimized or not, the driver that balances the car better than the other is always faster.

Interestingly, this granular balance manipulation will make you a smoother driver at any speed (think butter-smooth chauffeur), but it only really actually works to reduce steering beyond the geometric ideal line if the car is cornering hard enough to generate useful slip angles. In other words, you can always practice this in normal road driving, but the actual noticeable steering reduction really only occurs (with properly inflated radial tires) right at the limit. The almost ironic addition to this is that you probably won't consciously notice it happening other than that it feels good and fast, like the car is steering itself – sometimes the skiing phrase "carving" is accurately used. I really started noticing it on data systems at the Jim Russell School in Sonoma, California (now Sim Raceway). Data systems are amazing (if interpreted correctly), and in this case, you would always see the trend of the fast guys using less steering. If you looked down the running order, you would see that once you were a half second or so off the pace, your steering would increase, showing that the drivers down there were not balancing the car as finely. They were technically "textbook" perfect in how they were driving the car; they were good at it, but they were missing the few tenths of a mile an hour and the fine balance required to manipulate and manage that extra speed. If you focused your attention on their data plots for braking and accelerating in relation to their steering input, you would see how the fast guys blend the inputs better and to a much finer degree; their feel of balance was finer, and the data system laid it out in amazing detail. The slower guys would just look at the overlays in awe during the debriefings. We could tell them how to get faster, and once they were close, it wasn't about braking later or getting on the gas sooner, it was about developing better feel through upping their car control game. Those last few tenths of a second take a lot of introspection, honest assessment, and focused practice. What piece of the puzzle is missing that is affecting my ability to flow as efficiently as the faster guys? The answer could actually be anything from bad sushi the night before to a tiny bad piece of "code" you learned somewhere in your past that causes a minor surprise every time you access it. The eternal struggle for perfection inevitably continues.

Driver Aids:

In today's competitive digital world, automakers are compelled to keep pushing the level of computer integration into our driving experience. The advantage is sold to us primarily as safety, then as convenience, and sometimes performance. Who in their right mind wouldn't want more of all of that? That's how it's sold, and given the average adult's bare bones knowledge of driving, they don't appreciate that there may be downsides to blindly accepting more electronics between us and the driving experience. Let's face it: To most, driving is a chore, and they gleefully hope for the day driving is completely automated so that they can put their attention somewhere more important. Since you are reading this, I am going to assume that to you driving is not a chore at all, it is a privilege, and mastery of this skill is a worthy lifelong pursuit. With the bar so low for an average driver, it didn't take long for a computer to be faster than the average human. As of this writing, they are still a good way away from a good driver and a very long way from a great driver. If you use chess as an analogy, there are set moves and exact spaces to occupy for those moves; but when you drive in the dynamic real world, there are infinite variables. Driving perhaps has no more moves, but the spaces are not set; we balance a car based on feel, where in chess, they don't do feel, they do set moves based on specific responses to measured inputs. They try to interpolate and use algorithms to simulate feel, but they just react, while we do something very special – we anticipate. Take the digital music vs. analog music debate. The digital measures better, but the analog sounds better. Their programs may boast a billion calculations a second, and that sounds intimidating, but what we (at our best) do is anticipate the one correct answer: no brute force calculations required, just one correct move.

So, humans are awesome (phew!), but our cars have all sorts of potential electronics that can get in the way of feel. If you put enough electronics in the way, we lose that flow advantage and the car seems disconnected; in a strange way, they become better than us because they have muted the feel of the tires working (or not). These types of cars can be very fast to drive but are unsatisfying for the experienced driver. There are two types of automotive enthusiasts (and you certainly can be both): There are people who love cars, and there are people who love driving. The car lovers love all the advancements and technology that help them drive better, exploit the performance of a modern car and get better lap times, with the help of technology Contrastingly, driving enthusiasts hate technology in cars; they want analog direct inputs. They want to feel it all and do it themselves to earn that lap time – they don't care what is faster, they want what feels better. Now in racing we have to accept some level of this, depending on the series rules, because we simply cannot sacrifice speed. That is one of the balances that has and will always be struck as long as there is a human driving. Fortunately, the engineers realize that when you have a very good to great trustworthy driver behind the wheel, you should keep those systems just on the outside of the operational ideal for the driver. In simple terms, no intervention until the driver has made a mistake. Whether a car has ABS, Traction Control, or Stability Control, it should be calibrated to allow you to drive at your maximum and only kick in when you've messed up. If they kick in prior to that happening, we lose the feel (and the skill) to do that particular task very quickly and accurately, and become a little worse as a driver as a result. Personally, I don't want any system intervention, unless it's that "safety net" catch of something I didn't anticipate. Vehicle manufacturers slowly figured this out over the first decade these systems existed. We don't want to brake using the ABS; that means we didn't threshold brake very well, but when we hit an unforeseen patch of oil in the braking zone, we were happy it prevented us from spinning and ruining our race. So, after all the complaining, we have struck an uneasy peace with electronic intervention that allows us to feel and drive as the analog creatures we are, but with an electronic safety net just in case.

Electronic aids don't just have the potential to make us lose feel; they can also cause us to form and reinforce bad habits. The stability control system uses "intended path" to determine what to do. Intended path is where you have the steering wheel/front tires pointed. The system then intervenes if intended path and actual path are different enough that it can detect a skid/slide. In the case of understeering (front wheels skidding/sliding), it will add inside brake to steer the vehicle more. This can make a driver think and feel that in understeering, turning the wheel more will actually make the car turn more. This is absolutely untrue, but a stability control system can make it seem possible, because that inside braking while steering is of course decreasing speed; it is this reduction of speed coupled with the very effective single-sided inside braking that make the driver feel that stability control can defy tire physics. Adding steering to understeer is always the wrong choice for any driver; an immediate reduction of throttle or, if ineffective, a light but quick brake application is the proper fix. A quick slight straightening of the wheel (if deftly applied) can also help here. It is common to see drivers all the way up to Formula One add steering to understeer... None of them is great or even good at that moment.

Chapter 5

Measuring Driver Performance

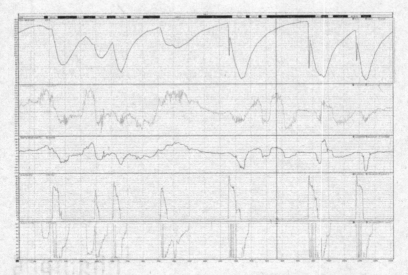

Typical data screen, this one showing (from top to bottom): Speed, Lateral G, Steering Angle, Brake Pressure, and Throttle Position

In the early days of racing, it was simply a lap time and a telltale on the tachometer to see if you over-revved the engine; you could check your RPM at different points, and you might have strapped a watch on a wheel spoke to run some segments, but other than that it was all feel. Today data acquisition systems have become common at any level from karting on up. They are a massive benefit to both sides of the garage: For the engineers, being able to quantify the dynamic nature of the race car has been invaluable, and the advent of seven post "shaker" rigs and now very sophisticated simulation software have taken what was a black art for a hundred years and reduced it (like everything else in our lives) to a stream of ones and zeros. The same can be said of driving–the subtle interplay of three basic controls can now be sampled a hundred or more times a second, painting a digital image of the art of driving. I mentioned in the Zerosteer chapter how I first observed that the fastest drivers were steering less than the other drivers. It confirmed something I had felt for years, and it was very exciting to actually see it on a digital overlay. Now we not only have the cars loaded with sensors collecting data, but on any pro team an actual data acquisition engineer (affectionately referred to as a "DAG" typically) on each car. Their job is to collect and collate all the data, and then sit in the debriefings after each time the car runs to make sure all the parties were on the same page and nail down next steps. On inefficient teams, there can be a contentious atmosphere in those meetings due to the drivers' subjective comments not supporting the engineers' interpretation of the data (and vice versa). On successful teams, the meeting atmosphere is positive with a real symbiosis occurring, where the subjective and the objective support the common effort to make the car faster.

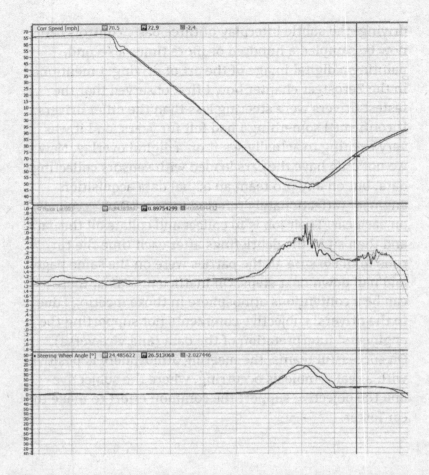

Zerosteer's Three Elements: Less Steering, More Speed, and Lateral G

When using data for driver coaching, it is important to understand that they can be a rabbit hole from which there is no real return. The problem is that data traces, no matter how detailed and accurate, only show symptoms. "Brake later," "turn sooner," "accelerate earlier," and on and on are what the data show and the bad coach relays, but what is missing for the driver is the all-important why. Without why (the root cause of the issue), it is usually impossible to get them to do any of it, and they keep repeating the problem. It's no different than my low eyes example earlier. Quickly the driver gets defensive, the coach chalks it up to the driver being a poor student, lots of money is wasted, and the situation devolves.

It is the interpretation of the data that is the key on both sides of the garage. Data in its pure form is completely objective, but as soon as a human is introduced into the process, it is up to the talent of those individuals to make it productive or not.

It was so rewarding interpreting the data at the Jim Russell Racing School in Sonoma. We had the fastest, most high-tech racing school cars in the world (and as of writing this years later, that is still the case). We had a simple goal of creating a relevant professional racing school. Even though racing had added data systems and they had become the norm, and even though racing cars (and even some road cars) had become aerodynamic, schools typically were still teaching in the cars they had used for decades. They all had some company line on how it was better to learn in what was now a vintage car, but it really came down to simply money. One modern racecar was expensive enough, let alone a school fleet of over twenty cars. There we were at Russell though, with an embarrassment of riches: 26 Lola F3 cars with 300HP turbocharged Mitsubishi EVO 9 engines. They could (and can) do up to three G's cornering and slightly higher braking, and they had full data acquisition systems on board. The students, of course, loved it, but to get back to the original point, if the person's interpretation of the data doesn't have a feel for the root causes for this particular driver, then it's all just expensive "smoke and mirrors." Don't get me wrong–a top racer can look at data all by themselves and make pure productive adjustments in their driving, because they have a process in place for assimilating the data and are not just trying to put a Band-Aid on a symptomatic fix. That's what the great coach does–they provide the process and the priority.

It all comes back to visualization. It's like a scene out of The Matrix: you're jacked in, so you can see the code. What that means is you have to visualize multiple channels simultaneously to see the real picture of what's going on. Cars and people are complex systems, and you quickly end up in a "can't see the forest for the trees" situation that is a true rabbit hole. If you have a coach looking at your data, you should always see them correctly predicting cause and effect: Too much braking or accelerating in the corner should see counter steer, looking at steering angle, and so on and so forth. You can't learn anything about root causes looking at one channel (parameter) at a time. The car guys are hopefully doing the exact same thing on the other side. If these two things are true on your team, you will be up at the front, because frankly it's pretty rare even at the highest levels.

Data systems are amazing, but it still comes down to the people interpreting that information for them to actually enable progress. You have been warned!

Chapter 6

The Foundation: Club level vs. Pro level, a cautionary tale

I mentioned some of the differences between pro and club instruction earlier, but let's take a bit deeper of a dive to see where the club environment often falls short. In response to people wanting instant gratification, decades ago racetracks started softening the standards for people actually getting onto the track itself. Clubs started appearing and renting the tracks (and carrying their own insurance) so they could set lower standards to get people onto the tracks. The bright idea was that if you controlled the environment enough, you could get people on the track almost right away. This has become the preferred norm vs. the traditional route of the professional school. It's much cheaper and you get on the track sooner. The result is that this has created a whole generation of drivers that have been trained to drive just below the limit of the car. These are the folks who don't venture onto the track when it rains. There are thousands of them, and they represent a great majority of track drivers today. This system under the flag of "safe, sensible track driving for everyone" unwittingly keeps everyone who stays from reaching their actual potential. The very thing that is skipped in the beginning that represents just a few hours of driving is the foundation that they are generally missing, and it handicaps their entire system and creates a culture that hinders real progress. It bleeds over into the way they set up their cars (to compensate) as well, which really hurts them if they ever try to make the leap into any form of pro racing. If only everyone had the required initial base of car control to build on... Sigh. I can dream, can't I? Also, after some time, they think they are above and beyond such basic training; they rationalize this by observing that they are doing OK relative to the other similarly-trained drivers and are convinced that the people beating them are only doing so by out-spending them or cheating.

As you can imagine from reading up to this point, I am not a fan of most club racing culture; it fundamentally misses the entire philosophies of flow and car control, not to mention Zerosteer. Let me be clear: I am not in this to have fun as my primary goal; however, fun is the natural byproduct of the experience of doing something very well, and that is the fun I crave... Serious fun, earned fun. I do support anything that gets someone driving or just thinking about their driving, but I want a culture and environment that nurtures potential greatness.

The whole idea of not putting someone on a track immediately is because it is overwhelming at first... Unless you drive slowly. However, if you spend some time in the paddock sliding the car around first with a real expert giving feedback along the way, helping you progress and monitoring you when you get to the track, you can really drive the car without artificial restraints, at your ever-growing limit. The pro instructor also shapes your form, making sure your priorities are in order and developed to a level where you are self-sufficient, self-correcting, and rational about what's going on out there. You are learning to be a car balancer, so you don't start messing with the car right away; you work on your skill set, and you learn to kill understeer with your feet and hands, not a shiny new anti-roll bar, and you grow from there as a driver. I mean, I love cars, they are awesome, but they are just the tool we wield to express ourselves... What do you want your driving to say about you?

Chapter 7
Braking Barriers

In my twenty-plus years of teaching, it always amazes me that often the seemingly simplest piece of any puzzle ends up being the weakest link. Again, this goes back to our own human nature. We often overlook something we categorize as easy, then assume it has no real depth relative to more important components, and lo and behold we create a weakness that can go largely unnoticed but has a real negative effect on our abilities. I say this because I have consistently found that even very high-level drivers who win championships and races actually do not have their braking skills at the same level as the rest of their skill set. Because they are capable of winning, it hints that the rest of the field in their championship also struggles with braking. This in turn tells me that people seriously underestimate the importance and difficulty of proper braking. Whether riding with people on the road or the track, or with students in a racing school, I see people subconsciously struggling and typically consciously unaware that there is an issue. There are a number of things to consider with braking:

- Maximum brake force varies with speed.

- Braking sets you up for the corner, not just by setting your entry speed, but also by setting the vehicle's balance.

- You are typically doing some sort of simultaneous downshifting.

Let's look at these points one by one. Maximum braking force does indeed vary with speed for two reasons: momentum and downforce. The first one applies to everything, and the second depends on the downforce the vehicle is generating. In either case, the point is that the faster you go, the harder you can break. Now, in normal driving on public roads, to be smooth you actually brake the opposite of how you brake on the track. If you want to be smooth, you brake progressively, that is, softly at first and adding pressure as you go, which keeps the g-force constant so passengers don't feel any discomfort and your coffee doesn't spill. That top-notch chauffeur may be butter-smooth, which is frankly great on the road, but they're (rightfully) not taking advantage of physics to shorten their stopping distance. The good ones at least do the chauffeur stop at the end, which is a light release at the end to prevent your head from snapping forward. Racing braking needs to be the opposite of progressive, which is "degressive"-typically a financial term, which means "to reduce by small amounts." Your target is "threshold" braking from the instant you apply the brake to the moment you turn the wheel. Threshold means peak longitudinal slip angle, max deceleration G for the entire straight-line braking event, decreasing pressure as needed to keep the tires at threshold as aero load and inertia diminish. As soon as you have initiated turn in, what an instant ago was right at the max is too much, and we now have entered the phase of braking called "trail braking." Trail braking is braking, but its primary purpose is not to slow the car, but to set the initial balance of the car into the corner. As such, depending on the car corner speed and conditions, we may do a lot of trail braking, perhaps all the way to the apex, or none at all, depending on what the car (read: tires) needs. So, to summarize, we do an initial hit of the brake as hard as it can handle, then decrease the pedal pressure to keep the tires at the edge of lockup all the way to turn in, where we will use the appropriate amount of trail brake (or none at all) to most efficiently turn the car into the corner.

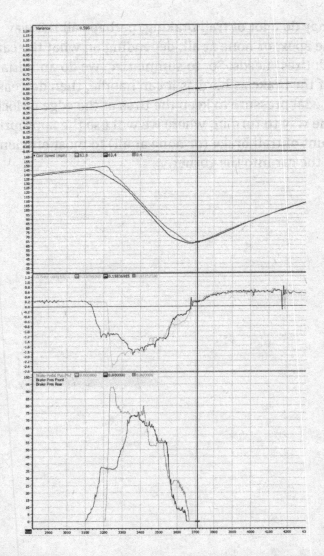

Progressive Vs. Degressive, considerable time loss due to inability to brake as hard, causing longer braking distances

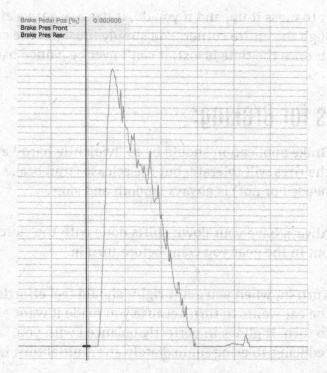

Brake Pedal Pos [%]   0.000000
Brake Pres Front
Brake Pres Rear

The distinctive shape of optimized degressive braking

You can see there is quite a lot of variation with braking, especially during the release; remember our target is Zerosteer, so our goal is always having the car very efficiently transition from braking to cornering. Simply put, the better we can nail the balance at turn in, the quicker the vehicle will turn, and at a higher speed, which, if things are lined up well, you will be able to carry the entire way through the corner. This is what makes braking so important and great braking so elusive. Of all the challenges to stop you from achieving great driving, it is this moment of turn in. There are so many ways to mess it up, and if you do, it has a negative effect through the entire corner. You simply must get the entry right; once the time is lost, it can't ever be gained back.

Tips for Braking:

- Brake application should be as "violently hard" as the tires will tolerate, but the release (trail brake needed or not) is always smooth and slow.

- Always have your down shifts done with the clutch out in the gear you want before turn in.

- Turn in, when you get it right, should feel effortless; the car wants to turn because you made it want to turn. It glides in perfectly balanced with you, reducing steering immediately after initial turn in.

With the infinite variation required of the adaptable great driver, it brings up an intriguing point about the difference between two distinct, yet necessary, driver types: The test driver vs. the race driver. Now, it is safe to say any good, let alone great, driver should be able to do both. One sets up the car and the other races it. The test driver is like a robot: They put the same good known input in (within reason) regardless of output (understeer, oversteer, lock-up, or wheel spin), and the engineers adjust and re-adjust the car until the output is as close to perfect as possible. That's how you set up a car to maximize its performance. The more consistent the test driver's inputs, the more accurate the engineers' data, and the closer they can get to the ideal compromise in the car's set-up. Then the race starts and the driver switches modes; the car's set-up is now pretty fixed (just usually brake bias, anti-roll bars, tire pressures, and wing adjustments at the pit stops), so the driver now needs to not be the rock-solid robot doing exactly the same thing every lap. They now need to be focused instead only on the output, continuously adjusting their inputs to optimize the output. The whole idea of our role being that dynamic car balancer is us in race mode, but the test (mode) driver balances the car and repeats the run exactly as the engineers tweak.

What you end up with, then, is an optimized car for that track on that day with you driving. You might then ask, well, if the car is optimized, why would you have to dynamically balance it? Boy, that's a cool question – good job asking it! The car is still a compromise; "optimize" means the best compromise (but a compromise nonetheless). That means that, at best, it's really well-balanced in half the corners on the track, and the car will very nearly drive itself through those corners. The other half of the corners are where you earn your keep; now you use your balancing skills to optimize the car as much as is possible (being the great dynamic car balancer you are) to make the car work well in every corner. The engineers get it as close as they can and we take it the rest of the way. This combination of car set-up as close as possible to ideal and the driver filling in the rest is the hallmark of motorsports the world over; it has always been this way and will always be (until perhaps the engineers get us out of the cars and we are just robot racing). The engineers are mostly looking forward to that day, because it takes the entire exercise down to math (which they love) and removes us (with our pesky irrational feelings that they hate) out of their perfect equations. That all sounds pretty negative, but it is half-truth and the other half tongue-in-cheek. The reality is that we need the engineers and they need us. What's the point of a great handling car if no one's inside to enjoy it? We can also (at the time of writing this) still outdrive their simulations for many of the reasons I put forth as the difference between good and great driving. The computers are still only good for now, and it's because they lack our feel and ability to anticipate.

Cornering

90 CORNER

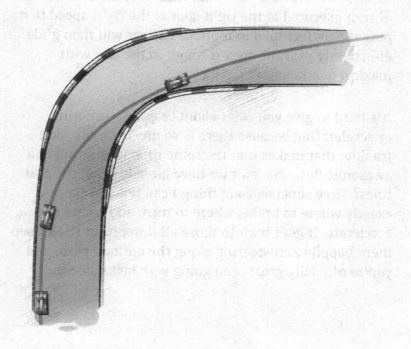

As discussed, with braking the most crucial point of any corner is a deftly executed turn in that allows the car to efficiently corner perfectly, seemingly by itself. Make a mistake at turn in and you will be chasing the correct balance and speed throughout the corner, bleeding efficiency the whole way. People generally say focus on the exit (putting the power down well) or on the apex (for mid-corner speed), but as I stated initially, it is precisely the entry that makes those other important things happen. It is the blending of two inputs that allow you to get the entry right, the release of the brake along with the rate and amount of steering input. In a really fast corner in a neutral car, you may already be blending throttle with turn in. In either case, it is the correct rate of turn executed at the right spot at the right speed that puts the perfect turn in motion. The car will then glide effortlessly past the apex through to the exit with maximum efficiency.

It's hard to give you rules about braking, cornering, or accelerating because there is so much variety, and frankly, that makes it at the same time infuriating and awesome. But... Haven't we have already given the real rules? They supersede anything I can tell you about exactly where to brake, where to turn, and where to accelerate. It goes back to those all-important tires; keep them happily Zerosteering along the optimal path, and you're officially great (and going very fast indeed).

LATE APEX

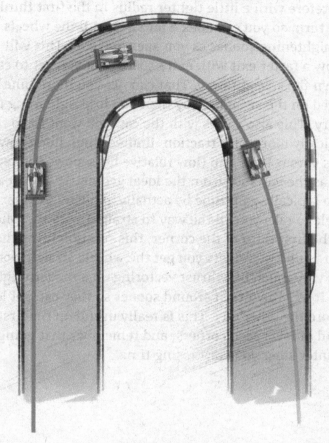

So, what is the optimal path? To state it simply, we want to steer as little as possible, as discussed already, but sometimes we need to prioritize certain parts of certain corners to gain overall speed around the track. In other words, there will always be places where you can gain some time by cleverly giving up a little less time somewhere else. Most well-known example: Any tight to medium-tight corner that leads onto any significant straight stretch should be entered a little later, and therefore with a little tighter radius in the first third of the turn, so you can apex a bit later with the wheels straightening sooner as you apex and exit. This will allow a faster exit with extra speed that you get to carry down the straightaway. That can net you more time saved on the straightaway than you lose tightening the entry. This also varies with the car-you want to do this typically more with traction-limited (high horsepower) cars versus high grip (low relative horsepower) cars, as far as the variance from the ideal geometric line. You can also typically gain time by actually allowing the rear slip angle to take you all the way to straight with the wheel in the first third of the corner; this rotation turns the car more quickly and lets you get the wheels straight sooner. It's very much like thrust vectoring on a modern fighter jet. It lets them turn around sooner so they can get lock before the other guy. This is really useful on the first third of low speed corners, and remember that going into counter steer you start losing time.

COMPROMISE CORNER

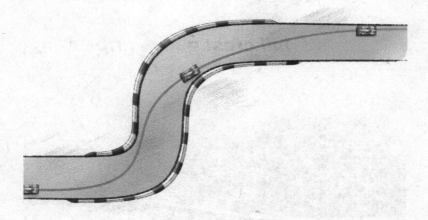

Another example is the compromise corner. This is two connected corners with no straightaway in between. Here we will take a super late apex on the first corner to gain radius through the second corner, especially if the second corner leads again onto a straight stretch.

So, generally speaking, we are willing to run a tighter radius and lose a little time, if we can at least gain it all back plus a bit, because the corners lead to some sort of straightaway.

UPHILL AT LIME ROCK

hill crest = less grip

uphill = more grip

We are also willing to compromise radius and line if some other area on the track offers enough grip advantage to offset the speed lost by compromising the radius. The most obvious examples of this are hills and compressions. We gain significant grip going uphill and lose significant grip downhill, and we also gain grip in compressions, enough so that we will almost always change line for hills and compressions, and bias the turning where the grip is, even if it is only momentary. Never ever waste free grip! I have seen countless people driving hills and compressions like they weren't there, always shocking and disappointing to see. Consider when I talked about the couple tenths of a mile-per-hour speed difference between pro drivers that it could be just that seemingly insignificant little hill/compression in a single corner that yields that lead.

We should talk about the rain, because that's the other time we compromise line for grip. First, let me say that you should love driving in the wet. It is free car control practice; you will do relatively little wear and tear on the car, the tires, and the brakes, and you will have a blast practicing balancing the car at the relative slow speed of rain driving. Anyone who takes the principles of this book to heart will love and crave driving in the rain – or the gravel, snow, and ice for that matter! Far too many people sit in the paddock while it's raining. As long as the visibility is reasonable and the track is merely wet, get out there! Back on topic: As for line and cornering, you should stay on the geometric line as long as it's faster, but as soon as it isn't, you should be searching for grip, because it's going to be all over the map from turn to turn, depending on the amount of rain, the number of cars on the track, where they are driving, and the consistency of the surface itself, plus the drainage. It's a cool little continuously changing puzzle, and it rewards people with great car control and an active mind who are always searching for a grip advantage a lap or two before their competitors find it. This is an experience thing, and you won't figure it out sitting in the paddock waiting for the track to dry. If you fear rain driving, your car control frankly needs work.

Chapter 8

Accelerating

There are two types of acceleration during cornering: acceleration that maintains speed (in longer corners) and acceleration that increases speed exiting corners. If the crucial entry of the corner was done well and the car is well-balanced and pointed where it should be, the acceleration phase will be progressive and proportional as the radius increases while the vehicle finishes the corner. If the corner warrants it (i.e., is long enough), there may be a phase where we are maintaining speed and balance mid-corner while holding the throttle fairly steady waiting to release, the car as we exit the corner. If you are doing some level of Zerosteer on the way out, it will be primarily your throttle application, not just your steering, that increases the radius of the corner to exit. I will point out that this feels amazing.

The Variables:

Cornering: All corners are different, we know that. It also takes an understanding of the car to really understand why corners are different. Now remember our Zerosteer philosophy is the umbrella over all of it. "Better drivers steer less" applies to every corner, but how close we actually get to "zero" (which by definition is the front wheels straight in the corner) will vary depending on the car, the tire, and the corner. Our goal is always the optimum slip angle for all four tires for as much of every corner as is possible; that never changes. What does change is what the tires actually need to be optimized. It fortunately does break down fairly simply and predictably. Corners can be broken down to three types, and you can draw a line between them for any type/ speed. The types are easy: slow, medium, and fast. Why the distinction? Because just like braking, the dynamics change with speed; the faster you go, the more willing the car is to change direction. That means that natural understeer decreases with speed. The faster you go, the more willing the car is to oversteer. For example, if you were practicing Zerosteer principals on an autocross course with your car and really have it down, you will have those tires balanced at the perfect knife edge for every turn, with fantastic results. With your newfound abilities and confidence, you decide to try a track day at the nearest racetrack. The average speed on the track may be two to three times the average speed at the typical autocross. Every low speed corner on the racetrack would feel exactly the same as at the autocross, but if you went into a high-speed corner and used the same amount of specific trail brake that gave you perfect Zerosteer into the apex of a low speed corner, you would instantly spin the car (or have to do one hell of a catch). So, what's different? Simply put (remembering my promise of no math!), the car doesn't want to turn at all-it likes going straight, turning is resistance, and the more you try to turn, the more it resists. That means it takes more effort to turn the car sharply (as we have to do in low speed corners). The more the effort, the more the trail brake required. Low speed corners require lots of trail brake, sometimes all the way to the apex, while medium speed corners require less (about halfway to the apex) and high speed corners none at all, with the driver on maintenance throttle at turn-in. Now you might ask, what speeds do those corners represent? With all the variables of cars and tires, the answer simply needs to be that you'll know it when you do it! The important thing to realize is the relationship between vehicle balance and speed and the need to adjust your trail brake accordingly.

The other point to make, as a result of the difference in corner technique with speed, is what happens to Zerosteer. The principle is still sound, but the slower the corner, the more steering angle you will put in (since it's a sharper corner). Because of that, having all four tires at their optimum slip angle for the whole corner will still have the wheel turned into the corner – it won't be exactly straight as my catchy name Zerosteer implies. The wheel will get closer to zero as the corners get faster. Great drivers will always optimize slip angle to reduce steering angle no matter the corner.

Chapter 9

Downforce
(braking, accelerating, cornering, car set-up)

So, now armed with an understanding of what the vehicle balance does with speed, let's throw downforce into the mix. It really is an amazing topic, and when these principles were applied to racecars, it really changed racing forever. Racecars had been streamlined for decades, but that was for a higher top speed. Once spoilers and wings started happening in the mid 1960's and the Ground Effects in the late to mid-70's, a massive host of options and new levels of performance took corner speeds through the roof and cut braking distances dramatically. It also allowed for tuning of the balance of the car relative to its speed. Measureable downforce usually starts occurring in medium-speed corners and builds from there. Think about that with the prior chapter, where we stated that balance shifts towards oversteer as the speed increases. With aero downforce also growing with speed, you can use the relationship to keep the balance the same for every corner. It reduces the compromise of having your car safe in a fast corner, but now with too much understeer for a slow corner. With downforce, you can have balance for any corner at any speed – you can see the massive advantage it provides. There are a few disadvantages that are small but worth mentioning to downforce. From a driver perspective, the big one is that you need "clean" air to reap the benefit. Dirty air is when you are following another car closely (drafting). The very thing that helps you pass the car in front of you (besides your mad skills, of course) is the reduced aerodynamic drag of following a car in the dirty air they are creating. That's all well and good on the straights, but in the corner, you will typically have a reduction in front downforce that can cause understeer in medium to fast corners; this is typically described as the front "washing out" when following another car. The other downside is that it adds a layer of complexity to the car set side, though, given its benefits, having it wash out occasionally and adding a variable to the set-up is easily offset by the benefits.

There is another way to lose your downforce: excessive sliding. Not that we ever do much of it, other than maybe a quick rotation on a low speed corner entry to straighten out the exit, but the other time we may be tempted to slide quite a bit is, of course, in the rain. So, what's the issue with sliding and downforce? Wings, spoilers, and ground effects only work efficiently when the air is going relatively straight through them. As the angle of the slide increases, the amount of downforce decreases fairly proportionally until the airflow stalls and you lose it altogether. This does not affect the Zerosteer principal at all! Zerosteer has us steering less on the ideal radius through every corner, which is exactly what the downforce wants. It actually reinforces the principle that if you go into counter steer, you have lost time and now we know we've also lost downforce to make the time loss even greater. I am hoping at this point you are really starting to visualize the Zerosteer optimal window where great driving exists!

Downforce and Braking

We brought up the term degressive when we initially talked about braking; with a downforce-generating car, the degressive braking goes to a pretty crazy level. Think about it: Because you have downforce, you can brake very hard, perhaps up to six times, harder (Formula 1 at times depending on the rules), but your extra braking grip is coming from that very speed that your braking is about to decrease at an alarming rate. So, the brake event happens astonishingly late relative to a non-aero car, and your pedal pressure is through the roof, but very quickly degresses to stay at threshold; and if the corner is a medium or fast corner, you are entering at a higher speed due to the still present downforce. If it's a slow corner, then you end up at normal levels of brake force (like the non-aero car) before you enter the corner trail braking. Just one more small point to make: From the driver's perspective, if your corner is fast but you are approaching at a high enough speed that you do have to brake somewhat, you typically wouldn't do an aggressive application of the brake, because you don't need to get rid of much speed and the braking event will be short-so short that a threshold multi-G brake spike would really upset the balance of the car just before the corner. Typically, a "brush" of the brake is used, which is a softer, longer braking event that will get rid of the same speed, but do it in a better-balanced manner. From the car set-up perspective, downforce makes for an interesting challenge. With downforce biased more to the rear, typically the amount of braking potential front to rear also changes with speed. A properly set-up (read optimized) braking system will have brake bias migration built into it, with more rear braking at high speeds relative to low speeds; it's pretty tricky to get it right, so there are many downforce-producing cars that don't take advantage of the extra rear grip at high speeds. It is a place that is worth spending some time and effort to get every bit of braking force possible at any speed, but still allow the proper feel and balance for a nuanced trail brake release.

Fitness:

Race car drivers are athletes, especially up at the professional ranks. Drivers are subjected to less g-force than a fighter pilot (who can see 9-10 sustained G's), but drivers face these forces in every direction, while the pilot has just positive and some negative, with the added benefit of a G suit. Then there is the heat. Racecars are very hot-in the summer, car cockpit temperatures can be over 130F. The controls are not fly by wire like the pilots get to enjoy; they are meaty analog controls that require real force to operate. The bottom line physically is that if you are in a high downforce/high HP category, you must have a multi-hour daily fitness regimen and probably a serious personal trainer, masseuse, and dietician, etc. All of that is considered absolutely normal and essential at any high level. Even a GT3 car these days is a serious neck-stretcher. Of course, sometimes the power steering fails or you have an exhaust leak or lose the clutch; you are a pro and therefore still expected to turn the required lap times for the full stint. It can be done, but you had better be prepared. The physical side is so important, because the moment we become dehydrated or fatigued in any way, flow is gone, and I might add that it is unrecoverable until your body is back hitting on all cylinders. Your fitness program will lead you to what you require, given the demands of that particular race weekend. It requires nothing less than the year-round planning of an Olympian or any other professional athlete to be able to consistently flow in an environment as harsh as the cockpit of a top-tier racing car. My three personal sports of choice are downhill skiing, mountain biking, and free diving. They all have enough parallels with racing cars that they help my mental game as well. They, like every other sport, are much cheaper than racing cars, so they offer cost-effective places to cross-train. I have spent countless hours flowing in my sports... Nothing on the planet beats the race car, though, but flow is still flow, so seek other avenues to keep improving your personal process. I also make a real point of exploring the potential to flow when fatigued by being very efficient with all my movements. The easiest time to attack other drivers is when they are tired. Try to always be the fittest driver on the grid. That knowledge will have a positive effect on your self-confidence, impress your team, and intimidate your rivals.

Chapter 10

Timing is Everything/
The Devil is
in the Details

When we add up the themes of flow, the importance of car control, and then finally Zerosteer, when they are all put together, we can feel the car to a level that allows us to truly have a shot at this "great" thing I keep going on about. This level of feel cannot be taught; it must be earned one step at a time. However, there are things I can give you that hopefully will help you avoid typical traps. We as humans love to simplify, to find patterns (the simpler the better), and ingrain them into our understanding as quickly as possible so we can move on to the next thing and make the fastest progress possible. Many of the bad traits that can become traps revolve around synchronizing the controls. The idea is to have all your inputs ingrained independently so they can also be unsynchronized; it is that variability that you specifically use to balance the car continuously.

Imagine you are juggling three objects. It would be easier to simply find the rhythm of the objects and catch and release them each exactly the same, and there you go, you're juggling... But... What if... What if the objects were different? Different weights, different shapes, oh, and you're outside and it's gusty, and your friend is juggling rings next to you, and you are tossing your objects through the rings – and aren't those extra layers of complexity what make you a great juggler as opposed to merely a good one? Adjusting on the fly while doing a complex task means you have to be adaptable, continuously adaptable. Remember that we like simple, so we try to simplify things, and that only limits us because we lose the nuance – and that's where greatness lives.

Examples of some things people like to synchronize in order to simplify:

- Brake and downshift (without some braking first)

- Downshift blip with clutch application (should be a moment after)

- Release the brake and turn (not trail braking)

- Turn the wheel and turn your head (not sighting the apex first)

- Accelerate immediately after brake release (ignoring maintenance throttle)

- Accelerating and unwinding the wheel (you should start the unwind first)

These are just a few, but they hopefully make the point that adaptability is the key to greatness. So many drivers continuously want to blame the car for balance issues that they should be able to fix while dynamically balancing the vehicle; remember that the vehicle is a compromise, and that great drivers fix the corners where the set-up can't.

The moral of this story is to never gleefully, hurriedly accept simple and then just ingrain it into how you do things, thinking "job done." To ignore the nuance is to be mediocre.

The last example on the above list is a fun one to expand
on. It all seems so innocent-we are, after all, talking
about tenths of a second differences in speed-but to
the car, it's everything, and our rush to ingrain and
move to the next thing left unchecked also glosses over
those little tenths of a second. After all, it's much easier
(especially on our well-developed egos) to complain
of understeer to the engineers and hope they can fix
it versus us looking at how we actually are causing it.
The vehicle is so sensitive that if we accelerate before
or at the same time that we start to open the wheel, we
are much more likely to get understeer. If we started
to unwind just a tenth of a second or two earlier before
getting on the gas, the car will relatively hook up and go
without the understeer. You are providing the available
grip the tire needs to accelerate a fraction before it
actually needs it.

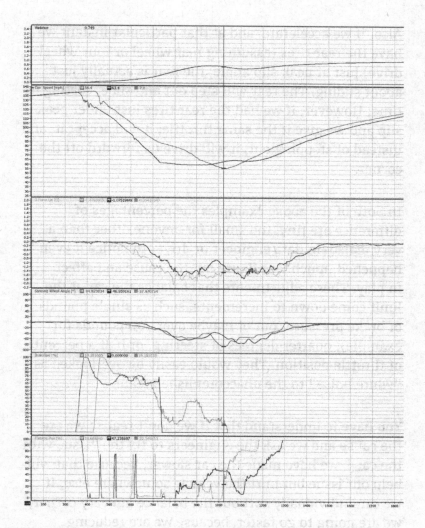

Early throttle relative to wheel unwinding slightly first often results in understeer, often caused by an inexperienced impatient driver who has over-slowed the car.

Also, if we accelerate, and at that particular instant we have the rear tires (assuming rear wheel or four wheel drive) just at peak slip angle, the rear is actually just about sliding. The rear will step out and slide, costing us time; However, if we had the rear tires just under peak slip and we give it the same throttle, it will accept it, and instead of stepping out, it will drive us forward off the corner.

In both of the above examples the percentages of difference are tiny, too small for anyone other than a very dialed-in data engineer or driver to notice it even happened, much less figure out the cause and effect in play. These adjustments that balance the car at the limit come down to increments, such as single pounds of brake pressure (out of maybe over 700 pounds for example), quarter degrees of steering, or half a percent of throttle position. They would easily be overlooked as "white noise" to the unaccomplished team.

You have to understand that if we don't realize we are the cause and we ask the engineers to fix the "issue with the car," we have made the car slower, because that will help our issue but hurt the vehicle somewhere else. If we can individually sort out the balance at every corner, we are going to go faster, because we are reducing compromise with the vehicle. As professionals, the last thing we want is to ask engineers to fix our problems. There are real mechanical balance issues with any car set-up without us adding to the list with our imperfect process issues. We should have all of that sorted before we bring up "an issue with the car"; out of fairness and professionalism, we should be as granular with our own self-assessment of our performance as we expect the team to be with the car. Once the team trusts you are bringing them actual car issues, the real progress starts.

The relationship with a great engineer is a cherished one. When the level of communication becomes transparent, the engineers suggest a change based on your feedback and data analysis, already anticipating that whatever the knock-on effect of the change is to gain in one corner, the driver can cover the negative in another corner to make it a net gain overall. This is nirvana in racing terms, and I can almost guarantee that any team with a working relationship like that will be at the front end of the grid.

Another point worth making is that for the novice driver, much of this seems just wrong. They will proudly say that they broke many of my "rules" (the examples above)... And nothing like what I described happened. That can actually be perfectly true(!), but the reason may be a bit embarrassing for them, because everything I describe in this book assumes that the tires on the vehicle are at or very near their limit. When the tires are below their limit, you can break every rule without consequence... Oh... Other than ending up being slow!

Part Three

Chapter 11

Anticipation vs. Reaction

This is a wild one where you can have very robust circular arguments with very intelligent people, because the lines between these things are a bit grey, to say the least. First of all (round of applause), we are amazing creatures with an amazing capacity for adaptability. It comes from our relative intellect, our curiosity, and our competitiveness, as well as from our emotional range. We can do both wonderful and terrible things with what makes us us. When you consider a supercomputer with artificial intelligence, it tries to fake all of our attributes using brute force calculations to come up with an intelligent reaction; at the same time, we pull in data from all of our senses and the sum of our experiences to be able to anticipate the outcome. We have a pretty good idea of what's to come at any instant in our lives. Driving is no different; as we build experience, we start to minimize the possibility of being surprised. If you talked to a great driver after a race and asked them if anything had genuinely surprised them during the race, they would say no. Remember earlier we talked about flow state and how everything happened within their subconscious adjustment range for every required task or they wouldn't have been in flow in the first place. So, what is actually going on there? When we are "flowing," does the slide happen first and then we do a superfast correction, or do we put in the correction in anticipation of the slide? Chicken or the egg? Hmmm, does it matter? Well, yes, if we are dissecting the nuance of greatness, it matters a lot. True transcendent flow would be the latter, a perfect melding of man and machine; the person who waits for the slide, no matter how fast the reaction, is still behind. You don't catch a fly with chopsticks by being fast... You catch it by knowing where it is going to be.

Think about catching that fly for a moment. How absurd it sounds for me to imply that someone would study flies to such an extent, perhaps for decades, to be able to consistently put his chopsticks in the path of a fly. The amount of trial and error, the false starts, the setbacks they faced until the true patterns of fly behavior emerged. From the outside, this person would be thought of as almost a magician, but underneath it all is someone with a very strange passion who put in the time and did the work to achieve something that from the outside looks basically superhuman (and more than a bit crazy).

It's all about process, isn't it? This whole book is about process, and understanding every single component of greatness and giving you an idea of how to assemble and assimilate those components in your process. It is so complex that most don't make it. It takes ridiculous dedication to the craft, a level of selfishness that to most around you will seem off-putting, and an amount of introspection and self-analysis that can leave our egos in shambles on a consistent basis. Done well, no one else needs to see or realize it though, do they? We can internalize this struggle, put a smile on it, and stay positive throughout. Think about Ayrton Senna, rightfully a legend; even though he was a hugely popular public figure, his life was bare bones simple. He was very private and introspective, he visualized furiously, and he never went into a situation without a very good idea of the outcome. From the outside, the general public practically deified him; to the uninitiated, his demeanor, his driving, and his approach seemed superhuman or even supernatural. Beneath that shy demeanor was a singular passion for perfection and a level of rational self-control. He put in the work...period. He made sure he was in the right car throughout his career. He was shrewd and calculating to an obsessive degree. He stayed with the team every night when they worked on the car hours after every other driver had headed out to party or had lost interest. He was dedicated to his craft and left nothing to chance. He was also paranoid; everyone who achieves greatness is. It's not unhealthy paranoia though, it is motivating paranoia, the kind that makes you have to outwork everyone. The reason for this is simple (and he knew it)... There is not that much that is physically different between the best and the worst of us; what we have that separates us is our work ethic and our passion. Senna was just a man like any other man, but it is what he did within human physical and mental limits that almost ironically made him seem superhuman. We all have the potential for greatness inside of us, we just rarely have the dedication, the honesty, and the process to ever see it come to light. We all are so flawed by adulthood that we have put countless obstacles in our own way-this way, we can have soft failures and be OK with them. "Well, at least I tried," we tell ourselves. Deep down, though, we know, and our being honest with ourselves starts with admitting that. Do you believe you have the potential of a Senna? Can you put in the work on your process that will allow you to reach flow state in the environment of driving a race car? Would you put in the work to catch flies with chopsticks!? The good news is that if you reach greatness in your driving, it pays much better than being a fly catcher!

There is something interesting about the perception of perfection, or more accurately, near perfection. I have used this example in my talks in front of groups many times, saying that great drivers make many more mistakes than novice drivers. I always get very puzzled looks from the group; they think my dyslexia just cut in again. I stand by my statement: The better you are, the more mistakes you will make. You have to ask yourself, though, are all mistakes equal? Well, no, of course not, they are infinitely variable and therefore cause infinitely variable time loss. A tiny mistake costs a tiny time loss, and a big one causes big time loss. So, what's the difference between the two? Recognition, and as we discussed, a great driver's recognition can be instantaneous. Ponder this: If you fix the mistake in real time because you anticipated it and fixed it as it was happening, did it happen at all!?! We would have to say that if there was a correction, then there was a mistake, even though the data may not see anything other than a momentary deviation of steering and gas or brake. Think of the novice in the same scenario – That same slide now slowly caught is also seen as not just a steering and pedal deviation, but as a speed drop with a drop in g-force–a measurable loss of time.

The difference is amplitude; the novice's slow recognition allows the tires to really break free, and that's a big loss in terms of grip. The longer we wait, the greater the correction that is required and the time lost. The great flowing driver might do several nearly unperceivable corrections in the same corner and no one even knows they happened. Remember, we are targeting driving all four tires at near their peak slip angle for every phase of every corner. The subtle dance with our tires at the limits of adhesion has the great driver continuously adjusting the balance, technically making loads of mistakes, many more than the novice's one moment in the same corner. However, with the relatively tiny amplitude of those mistakes, it makes you want to label them "adjustments," realizing they are just perfectly met corrections for overshooting the limit of a particular tire or tires. This is the sublime art of car balance that can occur if you allow flow to, well, flow.

The vehicle: You've probable picked up that I do call cars vehicles. I like to remain broader because many types of vehicles work in a similar way. Even non-vehicles like skis follow similar principles of how their performance can be optimized. We will focus here on cars. Let's take a moment to realize how cool cars are. Relatively, due to the massive size of the automotive industry, there is more money invested in cars than in any other industry. With more money comes more development and engineering. You might think aerospace or tech would be bigger, more advanced, or have more engineering, but as of this writing, you'd be wrong. With the size of the industry and the fun toys that come with that, the auto industry draws the real talent, and the racing side reflects this as well; the budget for motorsports eclipses that of any other sporting endeavor. The negative is that it costs millions to buy your way to top-tier driving seats; and if you do develop into the super talent that I hope you will, you will have to elbow aside all the drivers that can buy themselves in; it's as cutthroat an industry as they come. Back to the positives though: Cubic money. Motorsports has been able to dissect the car to an amazing degree of detail. Look at any other sports R&D budget, and then be in absolute awe of motorsports – it is on a completely different level. The top engineers in the world work mostly in motorsports; again, it's where the money and fun toys are.

Because of this, we know more about a car's behavior than that of any other type of vehicle. We also know a crazy amount about tires and their complex behavior. Racing is competitive, though, which means that although someone has this knowledge, whether it's shared or not is another matter. There is no Freedom of Information Act in motorsports, just the opposite in fact. It's a good thing that there are racing schools and that everybody knows everybody (and has usually worked for many teams), because this allows the information to get out. You do need to be very aware that it is all about competition. It is in no one's best interest in the paddock to help you, unless they feel that even with what they may or may not help you with, you will still not be a real threat to them. Hey, don't be mad, they sank a lot of money and effort into getting where they are, so expect them to play their cards very close to their chests. They will (and you should) protect any propriety advantage you find. Always be polite and professional and help when you can, but also don't give things away. To that end, much of this vast knowledge is proprietary; when you buy a turn-key race car, don't expect it to have any of the tweaks on it that made it competitive (and made you interested in it) in the first place. The seller will of course insist they are all there and that this is the exact same car that they are running... It is not. The things that make a race car win are cool little hard-earned "efficiencies" found in the grey areas of the rule book, not cheating per se, but things that the rule makers are not yet aware of and that if they did know about them, they would amend the rules to actually make the efficiencies illegal. Winning racecars live in the grey areas, and they are protected with absolute ruthlessness. So yeah, the car or the dampers that you buy from them thinking it will be the massive leap you need will be the un-tweaked version of that part or parts (sorry). This also allows for misinformation to be perpetuated: "Well, it wasn't the shocks (or dampers), I got the same ones they have and was no faster... They must have more HP, maybe I'll buy a motor from them next." Oh dear. Those things are earned or sometimes bought; yes, there is espionage, and there are breaches of non-competition agreements, etc. Wherever there is that kind of money, there will be all of that and more. Remember there are millions and millions at stake, and this makes some people lose sight of their moral and ethical values. There are many more good than bad, though, but the grey area thing is absolutely true. Why do they hire the best and brightest? To outsmart the other teams and the sanctioning body!

As I mentioned before, we do get a wealth of information that comes from racing schools that do research, retired engineers, and loose-lipped professionals in the industry, who often hop from team to team. There are good books from the Carroll Smith series, Racecar Vehicle Dynamics by Bill Milliken, Going Faster by Carl Lopez, the Secrets of Speed series, and the excellent software from OptimumG, just to name a few. I recommend all of them and more if you are curious about the technical side, but be forewarned, there will be a little to a lot of math involved! Some things are best left to the engineers, but some out there don't have the luxury of having a small army of MIT graduates to do the computations and calculations for them. It is also good for us mere mental mortals to understand the interactions of what we are trying to control and the ragged edge of adhesion.

As discussed earlier, it's the tires that matter, the car supports the tires and communicates the tires' state of being to us in real time. We fiddle with three controls to hopefully get reassuring feedback that we are well on top of things. So often we see the importance of the tire minimized or the nature of the car not acknowledged. People often ask me about the difference in driving a front-wheel-drive car vs. all-wheel-drive vs. rear-wheel-drive. My response is always the same: There are some small differences (oversteer correction with FWD is the obvious one, where you might add throttle in response, rather than reduce it), but the majority of the difference comes not from which wheels are driven but from what the front to rear weight distribution is. 60s muscle cars (which are all RWD except the Toronado) handle a lot like front-wheel-drive cars, because they too have about 65% of their weight on their nose, which causes a lot of understeer. It also causes really poor low traction surface acceleration performance, even though they have a ton of HP (which is why RWD cars to this day are thought to be bad in the snow, even though they now are quite good). A nose-heavy RWD car makes as much sense as a tail-heavy FWD car (which I don't think exists, thankfully). The weight distribution determines the characteristics of the platform; now, you can tune around it, but you are better off optimizing it for what it is and driving accordingly. What do I mean by that? The further forward the weight distribution is, the faster the car will enter the corner, because it will proportionally require more trail brake to mitigate understeer- "in like a lion, out like a lamb," as they used to say. So, let's look at cars with a rear-engine, where the opposite is true. If you trail brake that into a corner like a nose heavy car, you will get a giant dose of oversteer, so you go in slower, but the exit? Wow, nothing short of AWD comes off a corner like a tail-heavy RWD car. That leaves us with Goldilocks, the mid-engined car. Somewhere about 45 front/55 rear plus or minus a couple of percent, is the ideal compromise, where the entry is fast enough and mid-corner is good, as is the exit, which is slightly prioritized for lap time. It's why almost every purpose-built race car lands about there, as long as the rules don't make it uncompetitive by adding some handicap. Back to my point of how to drive it, you should adapt and not change the car; it is the faster solution. The vehicle should still be set up to have a balance window that allows for understeer or oversteer (therefore Zerosteer) in all three phases of the three corner types, so you can get on with your job as a car balancer. If you try to change the characteristics of the car by, for example, adding a ton of understeer to the tail-heavy car to try and make it enter the corner faster, you will always lose more time on the exit than you will gain on the entry. You are much better off trying to move actual weight forward by re-engineering the car and, in the meantime, driving it in a balanced manner, accepting its weight distribution.

That's why your job of being the dynamic balancer allows you to hop into anything and make it fast; very few racers can do this. Even some very good ones in certain car types don't have this versatility. They are only going to be fast under their ideal conditions. I bet you know someone like that, but again, that's not what this book is about; it's about overall competence in any car in any conditions and being able to give feedback to get any car you drive into that ideal window so you can get to work!

So, we want the set-up to allow us to balance the car in the three phases of the corner in all three types of corners. The interesting thing is you can achieve that in the same car on the same tire, and yet it can be vastly different in lap time and drivability. Just like mid-engined is the sweet spot for car weight distribution, there is a sweet spot for suspension set-up. Again, back to the tires! Always the tires, what do they need to be optimized? How stiff and how sticky they are, what did you learn from looking at the fast guys and talking to the tire engineers (knowing that there is proprietary information that will never be divulged), how much camber can you run in that series (if there is a maximum)?

Sounds like it's time to be a test driver and start to answer the ever-growing list of questions about how to get yourself in a position to flow.

A cautionary tale must be brought up on the subject of pride and car set-ups. I've seen this so many times now that I know it is a systemic problem in the industry. Set-ups and set-up philosophy become so cast in stone, and no one can really remember why we do things a certain way, but they are absolutely convinced nothing else could possibly be better. Now I realize that sounds absurd, and frankly, it is, but wow, is it out there. There is an important lesson that can never be forgotten, and it's a familiar one, because it is a premise of this very book about the driver. If there is a flaw buried down deep (and it doesn't matter how deep), it is this set-up philosophy about the car. It doesn't matter how amazing the science is; from that point forward, it is all based on flawed information. When you innocently ask them, "Have you guys ever tried _____," and they just shoot back, "That won't work," and then you respond, "So you've tried it?" and they say, "Trust me, it won't work," or "The guy before me did and said it didn't work," they'll sometimes even just make up an answer just to shut you up. You need to get them to understand that you are on the same team and that you need to feel these things (even if they do make the car temporarily slower), so you can wrap your head around the scope of what the vehicle is capable of. The not-so-good engineers will try to put you, in a box and ask you to stay there. A great engineer will look at you hoping you can together redefine the box, because you hopefully bring a skill set that will make the package faster. It is an expensive process-race cars are not cheap to run-but if the effort is to develop into a winning one, you all have to earn that knowledge one corner and one click setting at a time.

This stuff is where being a good diplomat outside of the car comes into play – put your own pride aside as well! Be respectful of the time they've had on the team and try to find some common ground. Err, hello? Winning races and championships ought to get everyone heading in the same direction; if not, you have bigger problems! The trick is not to come across as a threat; show respect, do not put them on the defensive, find that common ground, and never let up, because the car is never done, never perfect (just like us)!

To that end, you'd better either have thick skin or keep the Nomex on and visor down in the debriefs until you earn their trust. Just as the team can be defensive, we can be too (shocker). Drivers are typically more famous (notorious?) for their (OK, our) dazzling array of excuses than our driving. While I am human, and therefore guilty from time to time of a little "blame redistributing," I have really tried to eradicate it from my repertoire, because I have seen the harm it does. Remember, while I am a driver, I am a coach as well, and man, do I hear some creative interpretations of the cause of that session's imperfections. It is tricky to balance driver confidence with honest feedback, and a little diplomacy helps here for sure. Everyone on the team has a role to play, and for all of them, confidence is important to their ability to do their job well. The driver, however, has to feel confident, because no matter how good the engineering side thinks the set-up is, the driver has to be able to flow, and without confidence, it simply will not happen. The thing that usually causes the rift is grip vs. drivability, with the engineers saying it is faster (and they have the math to back it up), and the driver saying the car is hard to balance on the knife edge; in other words, the level of communication between the tires and the driver is vague or the set-up has a "peaky" window that is too narrow to consistently balance the car effectively. This is subjective, and it's not readily reflected in the engineer's calculations. The driver usually tries it and then gets the team to actually de-grip the car a bit to soften and broaden the peak, and therefore make the car faster. This is where the trust comes in, developed through mutually shared experience and, hopefully, success. With experience, the engineers can anticipate that their proposed "ideal" set-up might lack drivability; all the great ones understand the importance of driver confidence and therefore are very sensitive to making sure the set up enables flow.

I have been lucky enough to work with some amazing engineers, and their ability to fix a certain phase of a certain corner, while already anticipating and explaining the adjustment they know I can make in another corner to get a net gain, is nothing short of miraculous. The cars get faster every session in this environment, and obviously, we drivers aren't the only ones who can be great jugglers!

So, confidence is king, it's more important than all the data; but you better be faster over a race distance or they'll want you to drive the sketchy car. That is your job sometimes. Another example of where we might feel less than confident is when we are stepping into a new car for the first time. Most times you jump in, and if it's a sorted car, you'll feel at home by the time the tires come up to temperature. Other times, the car can be simply scary, especially if its performance envelope is a step up from what we are coming from. In those cases, we just need to "cowboy up" and progress in the car, and be very methodical and honest with the team. It's true they usually think it's cool when you show up and just instantly adapt, but they think it's even cooler if you are honest and don't risk wrecking the car. Make no mistake, though: They are watching how fast you come up to speed–it had better be that day. That is the expectation at almost every level.

In a successful pro team environment, we have a real level of expertise that makes for continued success; however, this is only a few teams in a series (out of many). What if we show up to drive a car in a mid–field to the back of the pack? To be honest, to me it can be really rewarding, perhaps more rewarding, to land in that type of environment and rally the troops and watch them get really excited as the car progresses and results start coming. That is the best part about racing. There is so much BS and so many egos in the sport, but... The results are the results, laps times are lap times. It's all so objective and quantifiable and everyone likes winning, so making the car faster in a less than front-running team is really cool and actually, dare I say, pretty easy if you have the principles put forth here as part of your approach. Remember, a tiny percentage of drivers really reach great flow-state driving. If you can do that, you will not be mid-field for long.

However, if the car doesn't work, you won't flow, so where do most cars go wrong? You might guess it has to do with the tire (since I can't seem to stop bringing it up!), and you'd of course be correct. Most teams put more focus on trying to copy the fast teams' set-ups rather than earning the knowledge the fast team has. The fast team, without exception, knows the tires you run in that series. They know how to bring them up to temp properly, when they peak, how they fall off, and, most important, they have a set-up in the car that takes every bit of that into account, with a driver at the helm of that car flow because the whole system works together. Most also-rans' cars are simply harder to drive and harder on the tires. Interesting point: The winning car of just about any race that has occurred over time is the easiest car to drive in the grid. That's how it is when you're at the front and you have your tires figured out; it all just plain works and that makes it easy.

The idea is that the compliance and grip of the tires is the primary consideration in car set-up. Tires are part of the suspension, so the spring rate of the tire must be considered. I get in so many cars where the car's springs are so stiff that the poor (undampened) tire is the primary spring on the car. Then they wonder why the dampers seem to be ineffective, the chassis is unresponsive, and when she lets go... Hang on, you'd better have lightning hands. Everybody wants stiff, but what they should be focusing on is almost the opposite: compliance.

Compliance means the package is as soft as it can be without being too soft. Too soft is when you can't keep the tires in their happy zone because the series limits camber (for example), or you need to run more negative camber than the tire engineers recommend. In those cases, the cars need to be stiffer, but only just enough to get the tires in their optimal zone.

If you are any stiffer than that, you are losing compliance and compromising tire performance. You are slower.

So, can you see the windows? We have one for the car set-up to operate in the tires' optimal zone, then the other, where we need the driver to feel comfortable enough to consistently balance the car to optimize all four tires continuously.

Chapter 12
Advanced Zerosteer

Chasing perfection at the limit is an amazing thing. With the knowledge of slip angle and the principle of Zerosteer, it gives us a balance or attitude in which the car is most efficient while cornering. While the tire is the priority driving style or preference/comfort level comes into play, we are now speaking of the limit in very granular terms. We know the tires' window of efficiency is when they have a bit more rear slip angle than front: It helps the car turn more efficiently. It is even faster than having the front tires up at the rear tires' slip angle-that's an odd thing to say because you would think the extra grip in the front would make the car corner harder – and for that instant it does, but it does it at the expense of yaw, so the car is not turning as well. Stay with me now, this gets a little tricky to visualize at first, but once you get it, you really will understand what the true perfect target is for the tires, the car, and your driving. The tires have a peak slip angle as discussed; under the peak, you are giving up grip, and over the peak (the limit), you are giving up grip as well, but you are now also sliding the tire, increasing wear due to excessive heat. There is a little window of just below sliding, then the peak or limit and if we keep upping the speed over and, sliding. This is where we want the rear tires and as you might have guessed, for the ultra-fast Zerosteer to occur, your front (wherever the rear are) are slightly lower for efficient steering because you are dynamically controlling rear steering with slightly more rear slip angle. Where it gets interesting is now preferred style has a bit of room here. The car's overall grip remains the same; the car is going the same speed as long at the Zerosteer is still happening. In other words, it works with the fronts just under the limit and the rears just over the limit, or the fronts under the limit and the rears at the limit... The car essentially has the same overall grip. This is really interesting, because I am saying you can drive tidy just under or tidy just over and you will go the same speed. Generally, the 90% that are trying to become complete drivers feel more comfortable with the rears just below or at the limit, not over, and then 10% prefer the sensation of the rear at least at the limit, if not slightly over. When you really nail it down, you will dial the Zerosteer down slightly in the high speed and increase it in the low speed. It should always be there, but in varying degrees, depending on what you can correlate via the lap times and the data system as being the most efficient, with tire life always being the primary goal in the race and lap time being the priority in qualifying, for instance.

TYPICAL SLIP ANGLE CURVE

*All four tires should be in the window, where
they are relative to one another in the window
determines Zerosteer amount and if those
intensional targets are different from one driver
to the other they are considered driver's "style".*

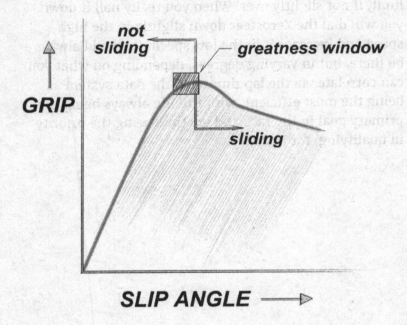

not sliding

greatness window

GRIP

sliding

SLIP ANGLE

Referring to our basic chapters on Zerosteer and slip
angle, and adding to that the advanced techniques just
described, you can relate it to your driving heroes! Who
were they? Think of Villeneuve, a driver with amazing
car control but overdriving the tires consistently past the
rear tires' peak, yes, he cost himself grip in the process...

But boy, did it look impressive. The other end of the scale would be Alain Prost, so precise and always within the rear tires' limit; and he was going head to head with Ayrton Senna, who sat right in that zone for which we all held him in awe, with a tiny bit more rear slip angle than Prost, and boy, could he hold it there – full commitment. Both of them won championships in equal cars, so either style and approach is absolutely effective, and you can see their distinct personalities reflected in their respective approach.

EXAMPLES OF TARGETS FOR COMPARISON

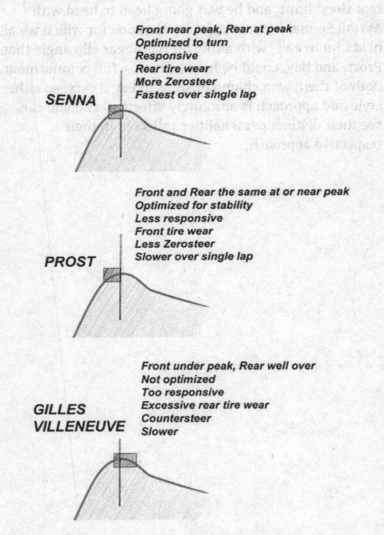

SENNA

Front near peak, Rear at peak
Optimized to turn
Responsive
Rear tire wear
More Zerosteer
Fastest over single lap

PROST

Front and Rear the same at or near peak
Optimized for stability
Less responsive
Front tire wear
Less Zerosteer
Slower over single lap

**GILLES
VILLENEUVE**

Front under peak, Rear well over
Not optimized
Too responsive
Excessive rear tire wear
Countersteer
Slower

Testing: We talked about the test driver mentality earlier (the input based "robot" driver). We flip that switch to drive in that mode, and we test as much as the rules or budget allow. We simulate everything from the race weekend to development of flow throughout the team (you didn't think it was just the driver that got to flow, did you?), and gain precious knowledge about the tires, the driver, and the set-up of the racecar slots in between the two. The very best way to test is on the Monday after the race series you're in (or want to be in) has just run, with similar climatic conditions and, most important, a fresh track (with new rubber and the right grip level) – oh, and you know the results from Sunday, so your goals are very well defined. Any other type of testing is still going to be productive, but doing a race weekend simulation on Monday/Tuesday post-race weekend is going to leave no stone unturned and have the least number of variables.

A fantastic example of this is what Audi used to do at the 12 Hours of Sebring. They were on an absolute tear, winning everything at the time. They would win the Sebring race, then not touch the car overnight and fire it up and run another 12 hours the next day. Why, you ask? To simulate the 24 Hours of Le Mans. Sebring was and is so bumpy that they knew that if the car could do 24 hours at Sebring, it would survive Le Mans. That's what it takes to be great, clear rational thinking, committed decision making, and, of course, well-practiced execution.

The Car is a Compromise until it's not (or How We Earn Our Keep)

So, we've talked about car set-up, how we, along with the team, come up with our ideal compromise for that track on that day, and inherent in that is some good and some not-so-good. The role of the driver is to enjoy the ease of driving the car through the good corners and to earn his or her keep in not-so-good corners. This is, of course, dynamic; even in the good corners there will be times when the car is not actually good: when the tires are cold, when the tires are old, when track conditions change, or when you have to go off line due to traffic in the race. These situations all require rebalancing. The entire time we are thinking about tires, always obsessively adjusting and readjusting to keep them optimized for every phase of every type of turn for every lap. We have built in every skill necessary, with a wide enough ingrained adjustment range to allow us to remain in flow state continuously throughout at-limit racing. This is greatness, and if we are in a competitive vehicle on a competitive tire and we (the team) have done a solid job setting up the vehicle, we will be impossible to beat that day.

There is a test driver/race driver duality to greatness as I mentioned earlier that truly great drivers develop – both sides, the "adrenaline junkie" and the analytically learned talent. It takes a great test driver (along with a great team) to ideally set up the car, then it takes a great race driver (along with a great team) to put themselves in a position to achieve flow during the entire race.

Chapter 13
Visor Down

There is a second duality: As a complete driver, we have both test driver and race driver modes, and then we have in the car/out of the car, times that can be thought of as "visor up/visor down." If I acted outside the race car like I did in it, I probably wouldn't have a single true friend and would generally be quite unpopular. I would also be a scary intense guy who would be tiring to hang out with. If I were the same guy in the car that I am out of the car, I would never win races. What gives? Racing is war, plain and simple, no quarter given or expected; never show weakness, be decisive. You are precisely taking out all of the politeness that makes normal life outside the car as tolerable as possible. On the track, you are either the hunter or the hunted. There is a stripped down basic "code" as it were – you don't ever do anything to intentionally physically harm another driver. Where the line is moves, blurs at times, and then moves again... It just depends on the circumstances and the level of instantaneous risk. There are only a few drivers I know of that are such bastards that they will risk intentional serious harm; most follow the code and can win championships along the way being very hard but ultimately fair. The ones that don't may occasionally win championships, but in my opinion they would have done better still if they'd been a bit more self-confident and not so passive-aggressive. You must have the respect of those with whom you race. There are moments when you will have to count on their judgment, and if they feel they owe you one for your negative actions, you shouldn't be there; so, whatever you did to cause that animosity would now be hurting your ultimate chances. Any real drivers will only allow themselves to be pushed so far before karma forces their response; a word to the wise, with more on this later.

Having said that, you must be ridiculously focused and selfish in the car; anything else is a waste of money and time for everyone involved. That means that while you're out of the car, every decision you make is towards that goal of you getting in the car the next time feeling as confident as is humanly possible. The reasoning behind this is that if you're trying to balance interests that are contrary to your own confidence in the moment, you are only guaranteeing a mediocre performance. There is no room for politics in the car or even out of the car; if that happens you just get into an ugly circular blame game within the team that makes winning impossible. This happens on some level at some point in every team. It creates a resentful "us and them" environment where progress is smothered by BS from both sides. This can be from friends and family to Formula 1; the well gets poisoned, as they say. I always say you should be able to add the phrase "because it makes the car go faster" to every decision that is made; if you can't, you shouldn't be doing it. We've talked about many pieces of the greatness/flow puzzle already. We are getting closer but we're not quite there yet.

Racecraft:

So why do we need to be flowing the entire race? Because, as complex as just driving the car at its limit is, we have another massive pile of variables to chuck into the mix: Racing. Testing is all about eliminating variables so we can isolate and progress individual areas, ratcheting up the car/driver/tire/team efficiencies to ever-higher levels. We know this stuff has to be dialed in by race time. We can't allow ourselves to arrive on the grid for a race start without having a solid racecar set-up and strategy. We should be only fine-tuning from first practice on, with no major changes occurring over the entire weekend. Even if it's your first time racing at a particular track, you should have previously tested, and as a driver, there should have been plenty of sim time. Racing is too complex and expensive to show up and wing it on any level. Odds of a driver reaching flow state in the race are pretty poor if we leave anything to chance by the start. Think of all the effort that goes into racing and how few teams are actually prepared to race when the anointed hour arrives. All of that effort for zero chance at flow. You might have heard the very true racing axiom, "A bad day racing is better than a good day doing anything else," and you know what? I totally agree, BUT it is actually shocking to realize that a good day racing vs. a bad day racing doesn't really cost much, if anything, more. The difference is in the thoughtfulness and thoroughness of eliminating variables in the preparation.

Flow describes the driver at one with the machine, driving at their very best with complete confidence and maximum efficiency. All of the tasks of driving the car at the limit are subconscious and automated. This is necessary because we are about to chuck in the variables of actual racing. Could you imagine being constantly surprised by the car while dealing with 20+ like-minded fellow racers!? That actually does describe the grid from about P10 down in an average race. They might not be constantly surprised, but they were surprised enough in the first few laps to know it wasn't their day and have now backed it down for the rest of the race. These guys lost the race in practice, with no plan or a poorly executed plan. Some teams race like this for decades and then blame the entire universe (besides themselves, of course) for their bad luck.

We're not like that, though, are we? We are rational. We know that flow (which is a very subjective state of mind), which can't really be measured, occurs only when you do all of the objective measurable stuff really well. Racing by nature is not at all conservative, which is why we love it. The smallest slip, the tiniest imperfection, will be pounced upon, exploited, and used to beat you by at least one other team. It is the unforgiving nature of it that makes it so amazing. We say that we are professionals in a professional business, but what we do is absolutely unforgiving and ruthless. Anything less would be frankly pointless. That's why how you race is perhaps more important than what you race. What happens between the green and checkered flags is all that counts towards success and failure, but what happens between the checkered and green flags (your preparation) sets the stage. We want to be ruthless, we have to be ruthless, but within that there are lines drawn, there is a code. As we discussed, we can't do anything to intentionally harm anyone. Think about that little piece of common sense: You have to race with these guys. If anyone gets the slightest hint that there was a deliberate intent to harm, you will rightly be ostracized by the entire racing community. It will not and cannot be tolerated; it's too risky in itself without some psychopath taking shots at people. Below that line, though, it gets pretty darn grey what can and cannot be done to win a race. It varies greatly from series to series and from year to year. There are three general rules that most series observe, and they revolve around passing. The passing car has the responsibility of cleanly getting around the car it is passing. Any contact that occurs before the pass is completed is the fault of the passing car. The pass is considered complete once the cars are 100% side by side (this is not a grey area but is the source of much video replay at the stewards' office to be sure, where the cars were relatively at the point of the contact). The second rule is that the car being passed cannot react by changing line when it realizes someone is attempting to pass it... no blocking, in other words. Third rule: Leave racing room, you can't run someone off the edge of the road and claim you didn't know they were there.

Living and racing within that framework, you have a lot of room to race hard while not intentionally doing anything that could harm someone. Your job is to confuse, surprise, intimidate, and manipulate, and that's their job, too. This is not easy. Think about this: You are trying to stay in flow and be the amazing car balancer. At the same time, you are dealing with individuals behind you (and sometimes in front!) who are doing everything in their power (with respect to the code and individual rules of conduct for that series) to mess with you. They want you to snap out of flow and get you to pay attention to them so you miss a braking or turn-in point. Messing with you is purely mental, it is only as real as you allow it to be – it's just like fear, it is only in our heads, it has no physical form. This is where grace under pressure comes in; someone may be the fastest in testing and qualifying, but in the race? In the race is where legends are born, it is how smartly we battle, how we progress, how we attack, and how we defend. We want flow to drive the car, because we need cognitive conscious bandwidth for the momentary adaptations we have to make, quick adjustments to strategy, brake bias, or the anti-roll bar. All of that can be done in flow subconsciously as well, but racing is racing, it is endlessly complex, so we continue to ingrain the next most important thing, on and on in a never-ending quest for perfection. This is a lifetime's work. You are in flow, and this allows you to monitor yourself as you are performing; it's almost an out-of-body experience. It's like you are your own data system monitoring your interaction with the tires in real time, making mental notes along the way to compare with what the actual data system sees as you experiment with line and balance. Remember I spoke earlier about how important it is to be aware in the moment? Progress is so much faster and efficient if we can make adjustments to our driving while we are driving. It takes a really high level of awareness to not ever repeat a mistake. Since we are at the limit of the car, we will make mistakes, but we should adjust instantly to never repeat it at that level.

Have you ever heard of our sixth sense? That almost
ESP level of awareness? Fighter pilots have a great
term for this: "Situational Awareness." It refers to an
all-encompassing feel for everything occurring around
you that can affect you. This awareness lets you peek
into the future. They love saying, "put your head on a
swivel" and stuff like that. Racing is two-dimensional
dogfighting, isn't it? They say never allow yourself to
get into a situation without knowing the way out of the
situation. That means when you are interacting with
other cars, it is your responsibility to have an exit even
though the other driver might break the rules (the code).
It's great that you win the argument in the stewards'
office after the fact, but your race was still ruined. The
more experience you accrue, the more normal all of
this seems and the less likely that your pace will be
negatively affected by those with whom you are racing.
That is an interesting phenomenon; we get so caught
up in racing in the pack that we don't realize we have
the pace to drive away from them, but trust me, your
team on the pit wall can see it in frustrating clarity.
Don't let anything mess with your task as car balancer,
running the pace lap after lap – that is, after all, what
you set out to do. If there are other cars in the way
messing with your pace, you must be decisive. You can't
sit behind them for any significant amount of time, you
caught them because you are faster, plain and simple.
When I say be decisive when you pass, I mean yeah, try
and surprise them, but when you pop out to pass, you
must be prepared to see it through. Have a plan based
on closure speed, braking point, turn-in point, etc. and
follow through with it! Do not cut diagonally across

straight to the apex; this is a desperate poorly thought-out pass that often results in a crash at the apex or a repass on the exit. You want to brake side by side with them with a foot between your cars until you reconnect with the racing line. You control the car you are passing if you are sitting right next to it – if you dive in early, you are compromising your corner apex speed, and they can still carry full speed past the apex, so it's no surprise that they can often repass. There is also no doubt when you are right next to them whose corner it is; they are less tempted and frankly less able to retaliate. You caught them because you are faster – don't compromise your line and make them faster than you!

PASSING

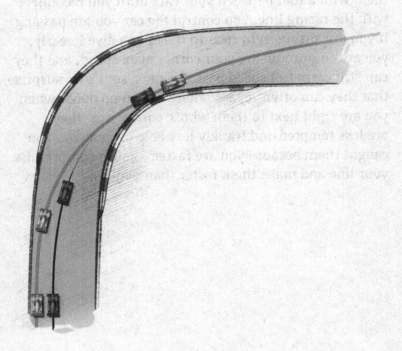

Once you have passed, focus forward; if the pass got weird and you slipped out of flow, focus forward to slip back in and don't worry about them. Again, you caught them because you are faster.

The moral of the racing story is that if you spend time worrying about the other guys, you will never perform at your best. If you are able to flow and have good situational awareness simultaneously, you can be a great racer. The more situations your racing (and sim racing) time can give you, the more capable you will be of interacting in a complex racing environment and maintaining flow. The goal still remains; no surprises, deal purely in anticipation, because we are prone to mistakes and vulnerable when surprised.

I mention the sims for gaining experience, and they can help. I'm referring to an online simulation, not a console arcade game, something where you are running against real people, not AI. It's not real, but it is so much cheaper, and they are getting so much better that the interactions between racers can actually feel pretty real – real enough that when a similar situation occurs in a real race, it might not be such a surprise that it snaps you out of flow, where, without the sim, there would have been more of a chance of flow being lost. As of this writing, the sims have reached a point where real immersion and flow can occur. The threshold was the latency of the system. We don't feel like we are really driving until the timing feels right; we are incredibly sensitive to any delay and it blocks flow from occurring. Spend your money wisely here and put your budget towards the system that has the smallest possible latency. VR can be cool too, but again, make sure the goggles are quick enough. Another point would be the field of view: The more of our natural field of view our set-up has, the more real it will seem. When you become an experienced driver, your sim time has nearly the same benefit as a real lap, so the value there is enormous.

I also mentioned having a decisive nature when racing and to make sure you understand the importance of this.

It is speed, consistency, and that decisiveness that gives you the respect of your peers. They want to know they can race with you, close to you, and that as hard as you are, you are fair. I'm not saying you should be out there to make friends, you shouldn't be, but respect is another thing. You can't race without it. You will find that when you've earned that respect, it will earn you friends in the paddock on every level and even fans, for that matter. You can't just be fast; you have to race well.

At the center of it all, racing is competition; you have to love competing and you have to absolutely hate losing, hate it to an almost unhealthy degree. When people talk about motivation, this is what they are talking about – people with ridiculous drive because they have ridiculous egos. They are clever, though; they hide the negative attributes very well or even make them seem like positives. It's interesting how you can say someone is obsessively motivated and it sounds like a positive, but someone who is obsessively competitive sounds like a jerk – it's all about perspective. I am a firm believer that there is a fine line between genius and insanity. That is where greatness lives, just on the sane side of crazy, just like your tire is at its best just short of sliding. You have to be willing to push yourself to a degree that is most certainly not normal. You want to know why greatness is so rare? The answer is easy: It's crazy hard, and just about everyone is too rational and too sane to put in the ridiculous amount of work, risk, and dedication required to achieve greatness. For myself, my real goal is flow; it is the happiest I can be, because it is me at my best. My life's goal is to be in flow state for as much of the time as possible, because it's by far the best drug on the planet. If moments of greatness are the occasional result, well, then, that's amazing. Like the hour meter on a boat or plane, I am ticking away; that hour meter measures my accumulated happiness. Racing itself is not a drug, at least not a very good one, but driving a competitive racecar in a professional event locked into flow state? Now, that is something special that I would say very few life experiences can equal and that the average person cannot even imagine exists. Steve McQueen was right: Racing is life... everything before and after is just waiting.

The End

Appendix

Appendix A: Life

So Mr. Cool Steve McQueen makes a good point on many levels. Racing *is* life. Now that's interesting, because when I figured out the process for achieving potential greatness in one aspect of my life (my driving), I almost instantly had an epiphany: *The process works in any aspect of my life* and it allows me to quickly wrap my head around almost anything. I had developed talent that went beyond driving and wasn't limited to sports. Virtually anything can have this rational process applied and see the same positive results. It also means that yes, you can flow doing just about anything, and that, ladies and gentlemen, is a life well lived.

Appendix B: Karting

I could not possibly add enough superlatives to quantify the sheer greatness of Karting. The ability to start at a very young age and to accumulate hundreds of races and all the experience that comes with that while you are still a teenager is a massive advantage. We talked about team expectations when you get that hard-earned opportunity to test your first race car with a team. That karting experience will greatly aid in almost every level of your professionalism... except one: Mass. Race cars (even Formula Fords) weigh at least twice as much as a kart. They also have slightly less grip and a worse power-to-weight ratio. This causes a lots of karters trying (in vain) to transition into racing by driving a car like a kart. Before that test, there needs to be a pro school/coach with enough days of testing so that the ex-karter (though you are technically never an ex-karter, as they are too fun and productive to ever give up), now driver, can now also flow in an actual racecar.

Appendix C: Skid pad Tips

Most of my description of the skid pad in the opening stages of the book involved using it as an example of how we learn. I wanted to take a moment here to give a few more details that were not relevant there. First, it is interesting to note that when training or being initially trained on the skid pad, you don't need to distinguish between understeer and oversteer(!); the driver just needs to focus on the intended path and on ultra-quick recognition of the slide. If the driver recognizes the slide quickly and lifts off the gas immediately while their eyes are trained on the intended path, there is no difference between understeer and oversteer correction. You will see the driver in effect just learning to keep the car at the limit. In a single lap, with some experience, you may see the driver make over a dozen slides and corrections as they gain feel for the car's limit. This compares to a couple of big moments (complete with spins typically) doing it the traditional way. Try it, it's cool! That brings up the point of time spent with understeer on the skid pad in traditional training. Usually much more time is devoted to oversteer (because it's more fun and dangerous) than in dealing with understeer. Excellent understeer recognition is critical for the complete driver (and my technique described above shows this). You need excellent understeer detection to actually get a driver to create oversteer, and glossing over that in a hurry to get to oversteer causes frustration from a driver and coach perspective, and usually devolves into the coach pulling the handbrake to make oversteer happen. Remember, there are no shortcuts to this; the driver must earn this feel one slide at a time, and understeer is just as important as oversteer, if the target (Zerosteer) sits right in the middle. I will again mention my method, it avoids this bias and has them attempting Zerosteering from the first lap.

I do like to continuously build and revisit car control training; as we've discussed, it never ends. If you think of golf, the entire sport is based on a simple swing, a simple swing that golfers practice endlessly, taking it to a level of art. Car control is our golf swing.

Appendix D: Coaching

"Coaching" is a very broad term; it can mean spotting, instructing, facilitating, and several other variations that all really should just be "teaching." As mentioned early on in the book, there are very few who do it well, those who really actually teach. Teaching only happens on an individual basis for a great majority of students. We all have different learning styles, and therefore teachers need to be able to adapt to the individual (not the other way around). A real teacher wants to know the individual student before they attempt to convey any information. Teaching a group together is really facilitation, it is up to the student to make what they can of the material; and very few can progress efficiently under those circumstances. This goes back to needing to find those root causes, and for each of us, they are indeed different. Not only do we each learn a certain way, but we have a unique perspective that affects the meaning of anything we experience. Teaching is only accomplished with a bond of earned trust between teacher and student. This seems to inevitably bring us back to the skid pad, or the Circle of Trust, as I call it. There is a growing trend in the industry for coaches not to want to ride with students on the race track. It a shame, because it is far more efficient to ride with a student, especially if you have real time communication with them via an intercom. I actually feel this trend has merit from a safety perspective, but I feel that this safety concern is caused by not spending time with the student on the skid pad first. It is the controlled, challenging, and yet safe environment of the skid pad that allows you to form that personal relationship with that student, to know their level, needs, learning style, etc. The student also learns to respect the environment and the coach. When they get onto the actual race track together, they are, at that point, only building on the established relationship. Trying to build an initial relationship with a student on the racetrack (skipping the skid pad) is very stressful, because it is not only difficult but also genuinely dangerous; there are too many variables, and they are coming at both student and coach too quickly. It is very easy in that situation for the coach to get behind the student, and at that point they are just a hapless passenger. I will also add that a robust discussion in the paddock or classroom is in no way a substitute – the Circle of Trust is where mutual confidence is formed.

That trust is most of the coaching story, if the coach understands the pieces of the greatness puzzle and knows how to help the student get to their root causes. The coach then needs to be versatile and self-confident enough to put the pieces together in the order that is most efficient and engaging for that student. If those criteria are genuinely met, they can be of great benefit in getting a student to their optimum level much more efficiently, and, therefore, more quickly and cheaply, than there could ever hope to get there on their own.

If a student isn't progressing with a coach and the coach just keeps saying the same things in the debriefs or over the radio, it's time for a new coach. They don't know how to teach.

Appendix E: Road

Road Driving: While this book is about a driving level that should never be attempted on a public road, I would be remiss if I didn't connect the two. I have also trained many drivers just for road driving, mainly in the form of teen driving courses. The main principles of not being surprised and having good situational awareness still really apply, as well as steering less (while staying in your lane and not trying to drive at or near peak slip angles). Your inputs should be super smooth as well (like the chauffeur), which they are on the track, but now we add a smooth brake application and do not really use degressive braking (unless it's a genuine emergency). One big point is that we are competitive, and we really need to leave that on the track. Most of the problems on the road today come from those clueless drivers that sit in the passing lane, but also from a passive-aggressive attitude from a large percentage of drivers. This causes crashes, but really, it also causes congestion, which costs us massive amounts of time and money, and adds to frustration levels across the board. There is a really cool book you should read by Tom Vanderbilt called *Traffic*. It digs into how we drive and what that says about us; it's a fascinating read about driving in the US. (You have to drive in other countries to see what's wrong with our road behavior.) With my fondness for root causes and not symptoms, here is one little example. Everybody who cares about driving knows "*slower traffic keep right*," but why do people linger in the left lane? Strangely enough, in many cases, it is the behavior of the people in the *right* lane that is causing this. The next time you pull out to pass or watch someone pull out, monitor what the person being passed often does. You already know the answer, don't you? Passive-aggressive... "Passive" is "I'm doing the right thing, I'm in the right lane." Aggressive... "If you pull out to pass me, I will speed up." This is not typically conscious, but is their subconscious ego pushing down on the pedal. Now, the person who is passing has a choice: Go faster than they are comfortable with, or sit. They often sit. If the person who was being passed had just kept driving at the speed they were comfortable with, the pass would have been completed and the left lane unclogged. However, what we often see is cars jockeying back and forth next to each other in every lane. It's all very silly and psychological in nature, and says a lot about what draws *us* to racetracks. We all (whether we care to admit it or not) have a deep down competitive nature. The point is, don't be like that on a public road, just follow the rules, drive rationally (remember, the other drivers are not trained), and keep the competition at the track. One cool connection to make is that great flow driving is about efficiency. This *does* translate to the roads, in that you'll get where you need to go, while consuming less from the car with less driver fatigue. That will make you a great road user as well.

The most important point about road driving for readers of a book like this is that the road is not a race track, ever. There must always be enough reserve of grip to account for the sometimes crazy circumstances that occur on the roads, but that are simply mediated away on the racetrack through strict control of the environment and design. Racetracks are designed for speed, plain and simple, and roads and typical road drivers are not.

If you have any doubts that great road driving even exists, please visit Germany and sit in awe of the level of organization, mutual respect, and awareness that allows traffic to flow efficiently and safely at amazing speeds.

Acknowledgments

Thanks to: Karen, Ian, and Rachael; Mom and Dad; and my brother Mark (who as my older brother was the target and my inspiration when many of these ideas were forming). Nico Rondet (an annoyingly dedicated and talented man, he was and is my true sounding board for cars and driving, and I couldn't have done this book without the countless spirited discussions over decades of working together), Tanner Foust (versatile, talented, and thoughtful), Allan McNish (super accomplished, intelligent and super nice), Steve Dinan (one of the brightest motorsports minds from any perspective), Emile Bouret (he can drive and he can draw, what can't he do well?), Chris Possehl (counsel and huge help editing the first draft), Chip Pankow (a mentor, the person who pushed me to develop most of what is in this book, also an amazingly underrated driver), Simon Kirkby (gave me my first break at The Skip Barber Racing School and has always been insightful and supportive), Derek Bell (teammate at Volvo, fantastic career and amazing man), Vic Elford (judging by versatility, most successful driver of his era), Peter "PD" Cunningham (fantastic dry humor, introspective, fast and open), Bruce Reichel (top notch driving instructor), Chris Baker (engineer and head of motorsports for Michelin USA), Sebastien Lamour (Sauber F1 engineer and designer of "Enviate", the car used throughout this book), Cody Loveland (owner of "Enviate"), Roman Mica (who gave me my break at The Fast Lane Car and selflessly made this book possible), Claude Rouelle (Mr. Vehicle Dynamics – his company Optimum G has global influence on all forms of motorsports, and he not only understands the team side of things but also the drivers' needs; it is this balance that makes him so successful) and finally Marnie Scheinberg for the editing assistance.

Dedication

Justin Wilson, Walt Bohren, Craig Perkins and David Loring. All true gentlemen who I spoke to about driving on many occasions, and who unfortunately are no longer here to share their considerable insights and wisdom.

Recommended Reading:

Flow by Mihaly Csikszentmihalyi, Harper Collins

Drive to Win by Carroll Smith, Carroll Smith Consulting

Going Faster by Carl Lopez, Bentley Publishing

Speed Secrets (series) by Ross Bentley, Motorbooks

Winning is Not Enough (Autobiography), Sir Jackie Stewart, Headline Book Publishing

Inner Skiing by Timothy Gallwey, Random House

Traffic by Tom Vanderbilt, Vintage

How to Drive: The Ultimate Guide by Ben Collins, Macmillan

Publisher's note:

If you would like to view the images within this book in full color, they can be found on Paul's author page in mango.bz.

Author

Prior to becoming a professional stunt driver, former Top Great USA Stig Paul F. Gerrard earned multiple racing championships and became Chief of Special Projects for Skip Barber — the largest racing school in the world. Gerrard has a wide range of automotive talents and deep history in motorsports. His ability to write and present in an entertaining and compelling manner has earned appearances on TV shows such as MythBusters, ABC Nightly News, Supercars Exposed, and National Geographic's Ultimate Factories. Gerrard is also a commentator at X Games for ESPN and the voice for the Global Rallycross Championship race series that features Ken Block and Tanner Foust.

theoptimumdrive.com

Also by Mango Publishing:

Truck Nuts: The Fast Lane Truck's Guide to Pickups
Kent 'Mr.Truck' Sundling and Andre Smirnov

Jeff Gordon: NASCAR's Driving Superstar
Jenna Fryer and The Associated Press